THE GUINNESS
BOOK OF
GOLF

THE GUINNESS BOOK OF

GOLF

Peter Smith · Keith Mackie

GUINNESS PUBLISHING

Published in Great Britain by
Guinness Publishing Ltd,
33 London Road, Enfield, Middlesex

Cover design by Sarah Silvé
Text design and layout by Stonecastle Graphics Ltd

All photographs © Matthew Harris (The Golf Picture
Library) with Rusty Jarrett *(p. 52)*, Chris Turvey
(p. 93 bottom right), Paul Minoli *(p. 193)*, Chris Cole
(pp. 208 right, 209 right, 212) and Larry Petrillo
(pp. 218–19) except:
© Allsport UK Ltd *(all historical material and
pp. 149–50, 168)*
© Chicot Agency *(p. 42)*
© Brian Morgan *(p. 173)*
© Jim Moriarty/Pinehurst GCC *(pp. 158–9)*
© Country Club Hotels Group Ltd *(p. 185)*
© Dunlop-Slazenger *(pp. 36, 41)*

Typeset in Ehrhardt by Ace Filmsetting Ltd, Frome,
Somerset

Printed and bound in Italy by New Interlitho SpA,
Milan

"Guinness" is a registered trademark of
Guinness Publishing Ltd

A catalogue record for this book is available from the
British Library

ISBN 0–85112–532–8

CONTENTS

PART ONE:
ORIGINS &
DEVELOPMENT

THE HISTORY OF GOLF

*T*HE EARLIEST recorded reference to golf so far discovered is an Act of the Scottish Parliament dated 1457 in which James II of Scotland banned the game – 'the golfe be utterly cryit downe and not to be used' – so that the population could concentrate on archery practice in an effort to drive the English from their two remaining strongholds north of the border.

Yet where had the game come from and how had it become so popular that it took a royal decree to keep people off the links at times of national emergency?

There are a mass of clues, a barrelful of red herrings, but no definitive line of descent cutting a well-signposted path for historians to follow back through the centuries.

Only in fairly recent times, as golf has spread its hypnotic hold ever more widely around the world, have other countries challenged the previously accepted wisdom that Scotland was the true father of the game.

Many of these counter-claims are ingenious, some are absurd. None stand up to close critical examination.

The view back through history is clouded by the fact that almost every civilisation developed one or more games based on the simple act of hitting a ball with a stick, club or bat. In some cases, virtually the same game was developed entirely independently on different continents; yet in others, small communities separated by only a few miles of rough country have been known to produce totally different ways of competing with club and ball.

The Romans enjoyed a game called *paganica*, which involved hitting a leather ball stuffed with feathers. The Japanese were clouting wooden balls in the first century, the French and Belgian game of *chole* can be traced back into the 1100s, the Dutch were engaged in *kolven* in 1300, about the same time that the Chinese were playing *suigan*. Then the French came up with *jeu de mail*.

There is little evidence of the exact form of the very early games, but they certainly did not give rise to any line of descent which carried through the centuries, and should not enter any serious discussion about the origins of golf.

Chole was certainly a popular game in France at a time when Scottish troops were serving in that country as part of the combined effort to thwart the English, and it is more than likely that some of them introduced the game on their return home. The clubs were very similar to the form of golf clubs, but the object of the game was for a team to hit the ball to a distant target – through a gateway or against the wall of a barn. An opposing team tried to stop them by hitting the ball away. Surely hockey and shinty historians, rather than those engaged in tracing golf's antecedents, should be looking more keenly at *chole*.

Jeu de mail became popular in Britain as pall mall, but the ball was struck with mallets rather than clubs and the object was to hit small targets or other balls over short distances. It was almost certainly the forerunner of croquet, but had nothing to do with golf.

The most persistent pretender to the golfing throne has been the Dutch game of *kolven*. Once again the clubs look remarkably similar to those used for golf, but their rather cumbersome metal heads were designed to slide a large ball along the frozen canals. This is where the game was played in winter – and certainly the object of the exercise was *not* to put the ball in a hole. In summer the game was played on small, flat areas, either bare earth or paved, rather like bowling greens.

It can be clearly seen that in most of its major aspects *kolven* was far removed from golf. *Kolven* has probably been given more credence than it deserves because the club was called a *kolf* and this was seen as a significant link. It is, however, merely a derivative of the Germanic word for club.

The fact that there was a great deal of trade between the Dutch ports and Leith docks in

A very early game of golf, with a 'steward' holding back the crowd!

Edinburgh gave further impetus to the idea that *kolven* was imported from the Low Countries to become Scottish golf. There is, in fact, no record of the true game of golf appearing in Holland until the 1830s.

Unfortunately this Dutch myth was taken seriously, even by many Scots, and a St Andrews author has perpetuated the lie in a series of playlets called the *Masque of St Andrews*, which is performed on an irregular basis in the grounds of the ancient cathedral. A sequence of graphic scenes traces the history of the city, from the bringing ashore of the bones of St Andrew to the foundation of the university in 1413 and on to the arrival of golf in the shape of a Dutch cloth merchant. The scene offers scope for pantomime-style comedy and much play on the strange Dutch accent. Better that it had been historically correct.

There are three key factors in golf which are not shared by any of the games which have been put forward for inclusion on its birth certificate.

It is played over large areas of land – no two exactly the same – rather than a prepared surface of specified size and shape; the objective is to get the ball in a hole in the least number of strokes; and an opponent has no influence over a rival's play, only over his own score.

If golf did not derive directly from any other game, it was just as certainly not invented overnight by a group of enthusiasts. Rather it evolved by a series of happy accidents over a lengthy period, perhaps several decades, and its final form may have taken more than 100 years to be decided.

The game was a product as much of the ground over which it was played as the people who played and refined it. The Open Championship takes place every year on links courses – for the very good reason that this is where golf started. As the sea receded from the east coast of Scotland it left great expanses of fine sand which linked the darkly rich, fertile farmland to the shore.

These areas of sand were easily shaped by the wind into rugged dunes and sheltered valleys. Wind and rain brought a fine covering of topsoil – it is still no more than two or three inches deep on the courses of St Andrews – and fine-bladed, soft, resilient grass prospered on the well-drained land. These marvellous links areas ran right up to

Golf being played at St Andrews in 1690.

the edge of many east coast towns and became the natural place for recreation, walking and catching rabbits, and archery practice.

They also provided grazing for a few sheep and goats, and it is easy to imagine a bored youngster trying to amuse himself as he sat and kept watch on the family goat. After throwing a few stones at distant gorse bushes, he probably found it more challenging to score a direct hit on a rabbit hole. Finding a suitable stick, it would be fun to see how far he could hit a stone. Soon he would take his brother along to demonstrate his skill and the two would take it in turns to see who could hit furthest.

The best, rounded pebbles would be searched out on the beach and a suitably curved branch cut specially for the job. They would be keen to preserve the best pebbles and would hit their shots along the clear valleys between the whin bushes and the dunes, making sure to miss the deep, sand-filled holes where the sheep had broken through the topsoil as they huddled together out of the wind and rain.

Gradually others would join in, bringing their own refinements. One would experiment with roughly-carved wooden balls which gave a much softer feel and greater distance. Another would bring a stake with a flag, which became the distant target. As they played backwards and forwards over the same stretch of turf, the hole where the stake was placed became wider and

deeper until getting the ball into the hole became the object of the game.

Soldiers returning from France might suggest better club design based on their experience of *chole*, and the bow-makers would have a distinct advantage over their fellow players by selecting the most resilient wood for their clubs and experimenting with different lengths and flexes of shaft.

With almost unlimited areas of linksland on which to try out their new-found skills, the east coast Scots would play out along the shore through the widest and most inviting areas of open grassland, then turn and head back in the opposite direction over the same stretch.

The number of holes involved could vary from day to day and from one area of linksland to the next. It is almost certain that the rules were just as flexible in those early days. As long as opponents in a match stuck to the same set of rules it didn't much matter – rather like nominating five-card stud at the start of a poker game.

As the game became more established, courses would be laid out on a more permanent basis. It is known that the early course at Leith had only five holes, but they were all over 400 yards and would certainly not have been reachable in less than three shots. Other courses had six holes, while St Andrews went to the other extreme with the original Old Course being no less than 22 holes.

In fact there were only 12 greens and 11 fairways. Golfers played northwards away from the city, turned round at the end by the estuary of the river Eden and played back down the same fairways and to the same holes. Those on the homeward stretch had the right of way, but it is not difficult to imagine the confusion with golf balls flying in all directions along narrow fairways between dunes, gorse and heather.

In this rather haphazard way, golf developed and flourished to such an extent that James II was forced to ban it in 1457. But, of course, it did not disappear completely.

The ban was short-lived and golfers were soon back on the links enjoying their golf in the same happy-go-lucky manner, where anyone with a club and ball could pit his skills against an opponent merely by wandering down to the links, establishing a challenge and taking his turn on the first tee.

There were no fees to pay, no starting times to book, no greenkeepers to complain about, no club fees, no committees – just a simple game of golf followed by a few glasses of ale or whisky in the local tavern.

This idyllic state of affairs continued for nearly three more centuries – right up to the fateful day of 7 March 1744, when a request from 'gentlemen of honour skilful in the ancient and healthful exercise of the golf', for a silver golf club to be presented at an annual event over Leith Links, was approved by the Magistrates and Council of Edinburgh.

The minutes of that meeting, painstakingly recorded in longhand, are carefully preserved in the archives at Edinburgh and they mark the point where the rules of golf were first written down, bringing formality to the sport for the first time.

The minutes read: 'It being reported that the Gentlemen Golfers had drawn up a scroll at the desire of the Magistrates, of such articles and conditions as to them seemed most expedient, as proper regulations to be observed by the Gentlemen who should yearly offer to play for the said Silver Club, which were produced and read in Council, the tenor of which follows.

'As many Noblemen or Gentlemen or other Golfers from any part of Great Britain or Ireland as shall book themselves in eight days before, or

Lanny Wadkins in 1991 – the equipment might change but shot-making skills are still vital.

Christy O'Connor Jnr finds the going tough at the 1989 PGA event. In the very early days of golf, relief was unknown – you played the ball where it was.

upon any of the lawful days of the week immediately preceding the day appointed by the Magistrates and Council for the Annual Match, shall have the privilege of playing for the said Club, each signer paying five shillings Sterling at signing, in a book to be provided for that purpose, which is to lie in

Mrs Clephen's house in Leith, or such other house as afterwards the subscribers shall appoint from year to year; and the regulation approved by the Magistrates and Council shall be recorded at the beginning of said Book.'

Mrs Clephen's house, which was to be the centre of operations for the event, was the regular drinking establishment used by those who enjoyed their golf at Leith.

The minutes go on in great detail about the conditions of play, numbers being drawn from a bonnet by competitors to decide the pairings, and the event to be decided by match play, the player winning the greatest number of holes to be the winner. In the event of two or more players winning an equal number of holes, they were to play another round to decide the outcome. In case there was any doubt about the outcome of a match, clerks were appointed to accompany the players and their books were to be scrutinised at the end.

The entry fees of five shillings paid by every competitor were 'solely to be at the disposal of the victor'. But he had to give 'sufficient caution to the Magistrates and Council for fifty pounds Sterling for delivering back the club to their hands one month before it is to be played for again'. The champion was also obliged to append a gold or silver piece to the club.

Having set out the regulations for the conduct of this first official event, it was then the task of the Gentlemen Golfers to formalise the rules of play. They were produced under the heading 'Articles and Laws in Playing Golf (The Rules of the Gentlemen Golfers 1744)'. They numbered only 13 and are worth examining for their brevity at a time when the modern rules occupy 75 pages containing 41 rules of play, 36 definitions and more than 300 sub-sections.

1. You must tee your ball within one club's length of the hole.

2. Your tee must be on the ground.

3. You are not to change the ball which you strike off the tee.

4. You are not to remove stones, bones or any break club for the sake of playing your ball, except on the fair green, and that only within a club's length of your ball.

5. If your ball comes among watter, or any wattery filth, you are at liberty to take out your ball and bringing it behind the hazard and teeing it, you may play it with any club and allow your adversary a stroke for so getting out your ball.

6. If your balls be found anywhere touching one another you are to lift the first ball till you play the last.

7. At holling you are to play your ball honestly for the hole, and not to play upon your adversary's ball, not lying in your way to the hole.

8. If you should lose your ball, by its being taken up, or any other way, you are to go back to the spot where you struck last and drop another ball and allow your adversary a stroke for the misfortune.

9. No man at holling his ball is to be allowed to mark his way to the hole with his club or anything else.

10. If a ball be stopp'd by any person, horse, dog, or any thing else, the ball so stopp'd must be played where it lyes.

11. If you draw your club in order to strike and proceed so far in the stroke as to be bringing down your club; if then your club shall break in any way, it is to be accounted a stroke.

12. He whose ball lyes farthest from the hole is obliged to play first.

13. Neither trench, ditch or dyke made for the preservation of the links, nor the Scholar's Holes or the soldier's lines shall be accounted a hazard but the ball is to be taken out, teed and play'd with any iron club.

What these first rules also reveal are some of the characteristics of the early game, for they undoubtedly represented the accepted form of playing golf at Leith. It may have been fine to wander down to the links and play without fees, but the common land was obviously a busy place, with people, horses and dogs having equal rights to enjoy their recreation over the same areas where golfers were trying to hit the ball as far as possible – about 200 yards representing a good shot by a proficient player at that time.

The fact that the tee shot had to be made

within one club's length of the previous hole speaks volumes for the state of the greens. They were not prepared like billiard tables in the modern manner, but were just reasonably flat areas in convenient locations.

The ball was normally teed up on a small pile of sand, which each player would take from the bottom of the hole after putting out. There was no stipulated size for the hole, but it obviously got much deeper and wider as play went on.

The second rule – 'your tee must be upon the ground' – does not seem to make much sense if the tee is a pile of sand. But in some old illustrations of the Dutch *kolven*, players have taken advantage of a fallen tree branch or exposed root to tee the ball above ground level, so presumably this rule was designed to prevent such malpractice.

The Gentlemen Golfers of Leith certainly started something with their rules and their annual tournament. There is no evidence of any other gathering of golfers forming themselves into a club or society before Leith made their mark in 1744, and they must therefore be regarded as the oldest golf club.

They eventually moved away from the crowded links of Leith and spent some years based at Musselburgh before creating their own championship course at Muirfield in 1891. Long before this time they had adopted the name 'The Honourable Company of Edinburgh Golfers'.

One counter claim for the title of the oldest golf club comes, strangely, from Royal Blackheath in London. In the *Golfer's Handbook* the club is listed as 'instituted traditionally in 1608'. This claim relies on the notion that James VI of Scotland, on becoming James I of England and moving south to take up residence in London in 1603, took his interest in the game with him. Yet the first silver club was not played for at Blackheath until 1766, and there is not one shred of written evidence to suggest that the club was formed before that date.

The Royal Burgess Club in Edinburgh, undoubtedly one of the oldest, has already celebrated its 250th anniversary, but there is no documented proof that it was formalised as a club until the 1770s. When the Society of St Andrews Golfers bought their first silver club and started life in 1754, they used the same 13 basic rules laid

down in Edinburgh 10 years before. This was the club that was later to become the Royal and Ancient Golf Club of St Andrews – the governing body of world golf.

Parading the Silver Club of the Honourable Company of Edinburgh Golfers in the 18th century.

EVEN before the first clubs were formed, golf was always a very sociable game. An inn or tavern could be found close by where triumphant and defeated golfers alike would retire for a little light refreshment. If no tavern existed, one would soon open up to cater for the sometimes extravagant demands of the golfers.

The early clubs and societies conducted their meetings and held their dinners at the nearest tavern, long before they were ever in a position to build their own clubhouses.

The records of the Royal Burgess in Edinburgh reveal a great deal of what a club member could expect in the late 1700s. A young servant was employed by the club for six shillings a quarter and given a suit of clothes which was only to be worn on Saturday and Sunday. His first job on Saturday morning was to call at the house of every member and enquire whether they wished to dine in their private room at the Golf Tavern that evening.

William Inglis, Captain of the Honourable Company of Edinburgh Golfers, 1787.

Once the outcome of the match was decided, the protagonists would join their fellow golfers to enjoy a few pints of ale before settling down to the more serious business of the evening. Each match during the day would have been played for a wager – which was much more likely to be a flagon of wine or a gallon of brandy than any monetary amount.

These debts would be settled at dinner and almost certainly opened if not finished. Accounts of mammoth eating and drinking excesses are common and Tobias Smollett wrote that club golfers rarely retired to bed with less than a gallon of claret in their bellies. Meals would typically consist of venison, beef, mutton, pigeon or pheasant and everyone had a serious helping of each.

During the meal, matches would be arranged for the following week and as the evening wore on, the wagers became more extravagant. By tradition the club captain was the man who had won the annual championship, and he would preside at dinner, instructing the club recorder to announce the results of the day's matches and note down the increasingly incoherent wagers for the following weekend.

Although the scale of post-match entertainment and hospitality has diminished over the years, the basic conviviality and sociability associated with golf has, to a large extent, survived the massive expansion of the game across countries and continents.

That expansion started slowly enough, the game having been played for something close to 400 years in its birthplace on the east coast of Scotland before expanding west and south, to Prestwick where the Open Championship was first played, and to London and Manchester.

There were only three English clubs by the 1860s, compared to more than 30 in Scotland, but travel was becoming easier as the railway network expanded, and a significant change in the manufacture of the golf ball had a dynamic effect, both on the popularity of golf and the design of the clubs with which it was played.

Until 1848 golf balls were made by a very slow and difficult process. Pieces of shaped bull's hide were soaked in alum water and stitched together, leaving a small hole through which a mass of boiled goose feathers were stuffed. As the

During the afternoon he would act as a caddy, probably for the club captain, and at night he served at table. Some ten years after he was first appointed he was also given a pair of shoes at the club's expense 'on account of the large increase of members which occasioned a great deal of additional walking.'

In those days the members played over Bruntsfield Links, then on the southern edge of Edinburgh under the shadow of the castle, now effectively in the heart of the city and preserved as a small par-three course and still overlooked by the Golf Tavern, which was built in 1456.

Members played always in their scarlet coats – there were sizeable fines for those who failed to observe the rule – and caddies would carry the clubs in a loose bundle under their arms, with a supply of golf balls stored in various pockets about their person. Golf bags had not yet been invented. The game would be decided by match-play and there were bound to be numerous delays as people walked and rode across the common land.

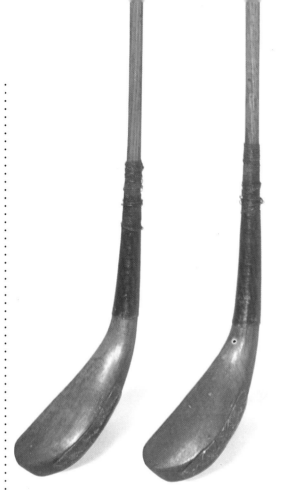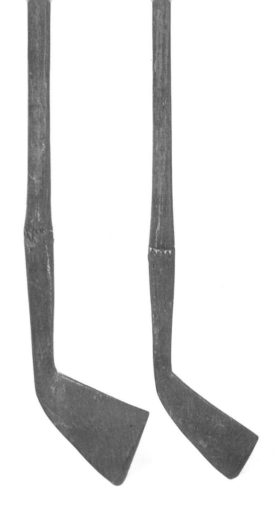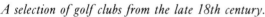

A selection of golf clubs from the late 18th century.

filling became more and more solid, the skilled ball-maker would have to use a metal rod strapped to his chest or under the arm to exert more pressure. As the feathers dried out they expanded, while the leather shrank.

The Romans had used exactly the same method to make balls for their game of *paganica* – and the result was excellent, solid yet resilient, if not very durable. It was such a tricky procedure, however, that even the most skilled ball-makers like Allan Robertson in St Andrews could produce no more than six a day, and four was closer to the average. They were consequently expensive.

In dry conditions they lasted reasonably well, but in the wet they were liable to split open at any moment. It was difficult for ball-makers to keep pace with demand – despite the high prices.

A tough, rubbery substance called gutta percha was to change all that almost overnight. Heated and clamped into moulds, it produced perfectly round, almost indestructible golf balls in minutes. But it was not to prove quite as simple as that. A perfectly smooth 'guttie' ball, as they quickly became known, was a great disappointment.

It simply did not fly as well as expected, but it got better as the surface became scuffed and worn.

The old 'featherie' balls had slightly raised, stitched seams which gave them lift, and as soon as makers of the guttie started to mould the new balls with raised or indented patterns, they achieved the desired results.

The new ball made golf more accessible and more enjoyable, but it inevitably had far-reaching effects on the way golf clubs were designed and made. The featherie ball had been fairly light and soft. Golf clubs mostly had long, slender, shallow wooden heads at the end of lengthy, supple shafts. The new ball felt hard and soon started to damage clubheads. Inserts of leather and horn were put into the club faces to stop the wear, and gradually the shape of the heads became shorter and deeper to cope with the heavier impact.

A retired Navy captain living in St Andrews was constantly experimenting with gutta percha, adding ground cork or iron filings to the mixture before moulding the balls. He was not interested in commercial production, turning out only a few balls at a time for use by his golfing friends. One

HASKELL ROYAL 2/- **EACH**

OF ALL DEALERS
AND PROFESSIONALS
OR FROM
THE SOLE MANUFACTURERS
THE **B.F. GOODRICH Co.**
7, SNOW HILL, LONDON, E.C.

A sample ball sent post free on
receipt of P.O. value 2/- from
the manufacturers.

"I must have his name & address – he's driven beyond the limit."

Above: *Extravagant claims would appear to be nothing new in advertising.*

AN IDEAL COMBINATION
OF
SPEED-FLIGHT
AND
DURABILITY.

THE
HASKELL
"No. 10."

OF ALL
DEALERS
per **24/-**
AND
PROFESSIONALS
doz.

Manufactured only by
THE **B. F. GOODRICH CO.,**
7, Snow Hill, E.C.

J. B. HALLEY, Distributor, 16, Finsbury Circus, E.C.

Right: *The Haskell ball was highly popular at the turn of the century – though far from cheap.*

of his most successful experiments was to wind yards of rubber round a core of gutta percha and then to mould another layer of gutta percha around the outside as a cover. But he moved away from St Andrews in 1879 and gave up golf.

It was another 30 years before the American Coburn Haskell invented a ball which featured rubber windings around a central core, with a cover of gutta percha. It became an immediate success and earned him a fortune. In essence it is the same ball which is played with today.

Sandy Herd paid an exorbitant price for one of the first rubber-cored balls to be brought into Britain and he used it to devastating effect to win the 1902 Open Championship. Modern profession-

als will use a new ball every two or three holes in tournament play, in their constant search for perfection. Herd made his one Haskell ball last for 72 holes, but it was in considerably less than perfect condition by the end of the championship.

These two significant changes in the golf ball were matched by two equally important developments in the materials used for golf club shafts. Blackthorn and hazel were commonly used in the early days of the game, before the excellent properties of American hickory were introduced to Scotland in about 1825. Its tough, resilient, springy qualities were perfect for golf club shafts and by the turn of the century massive quantities were being imported. Spalding advertised the arrival of a quarter of a million shafts which they were offering to clubmakers in lots of between 1000 and 10 000.

Hickory reigned supreme for 100 years, until technology advanced to the point where tubular steel could be produced with walls thin and light enough to make it the ideal choice for club shafts.

Sandy Herd, winner of the 1902 British Open, was dedicated to the Haskell.

All the disadvantages of wooden shafts were immediately overcome. Apart from the obvious fact that they could break at any time, they had to be stored in conditions that were not too hot or dry, and replacing a broken shaft with one giving similar feel and flex was very much a hit-and-miss affair. Skilled clubmakers would spend hours shaving and whittling lengths of hickory to achieve the desired results.

Steel tubing could be mass-produced and was virtually unbreakable, but many golfers who had played throughout their lives with hickory shafts believed that the move to steel took much of the feel and finesse out of the game.

It was certainly responsible for changing the shape of the golf swing. In its formative years, golf was played with long-shafted clubs with a very wide angle between shaft and clubhead. The stance was open and the ball was swept off the turf with a very flat, round-the-body swing. The ball did not rise very high in the air and the ground was generally hard and fast-running so that quite respectable drives of 200 yards were not uncommon. But there was no way that the ball could be floated high in the air over a bunker and stopped on a bone-hard green.

In many ways the game was more demanding then. Today's tournament professionals can hit the ball 30 yards off line and then smash a wedge shot over any intervening trouble to a well-watered green and make the ball screw to a stop. Their golfing ancestors had to be precise with their tee shots in order to be able to run the ball between bunkers and bushes towards the flag. The high-flying aerial route was not an available option.

As the softer wooden shafts gave way to hickory, and gutta percha produced a harder, more solid ball, so the heads of the clubs became larger, shafts were shortened and the angle between shaft and clubhead was reduced, leading to a more upright swing.

This process was continued through the development of the rubber-cored ball and the steel shaft until the whole perception of the game had changed from one where the ball was swept away, barely bruising the grass, to the upright modern swing where the object is to hit firmly down through the ball, taking divots large enough to make a new lawn.

DESPITE the limitations of the early equipment, the standard was often very high. The five original holes at Leith were all over 400 yards, with one just short of 500, and the average scores in competition were about six strokes per hole.

When Willie Park of Musselburgh won the first Open Championship at Prestwick in 1860, the event was played as three rounds of the 12-hole course. In extremely bad weather his score of

174, equivalent to a pair of 87s, was a very creditable performance and gave him victory by two shots over Old Tom Morris. The following year Tom was to gain his revenge with a score of 163 and by the time his son – Young Tom – captured the title for the third consecutive year in 1870, his winning score had dropped to 149, or the equal of rounds of 74 and 75.

Until that time most competition took the form of big-money matches. Willie Dunn played St Andrews professional Allan Robertson in a 20-round match in 1843 and lost the £100 wager by two rounds with one to play. Robertson was reputed never to have lost a singles match, but he was also accused of choosing his opponents with extreme caution. Regarded as the first professional, he was a skilled maker of featherie balls and tried to obstruct the introduction of the gutta percha ball. He went as far as buying up existing stocks and paid caddies to bring him any gutties they found on the links. He burned the offending balls but failed to stand in the way of progress. He died two years before the first Open Championship.

Old Tom Morris (knees bent) was taught golf and clubmaking by Allan Robertson, pictured with him here.

His one-time apprentice, Old Tom Morris – they parted company in a row about guttie balls – was also a great match player and joined forces with his brilliant son, Young Tom, to win many a wager. It was during a match at North Berwick against the brothers Willie and Mungo Park that a telegram arrived with news that Young Tom's wife was dangerously ill in childbirth. The news was kept from him until the end of the match and although a yacht was put at his disposal to save time by sailing directly across the Forth estuary back to St Andrews, his wife had died by the time he stepped ashore.

The romantic version is that he died of a broken heart on Christmas Day of that same year, 1875, at the age of 24. The truth is that he tried to allay his deep grief with whisky. He had been awarded the original Open Championship trophy – a Moroccan leather belt with a large silver buckle – for winning the title three years in a row, and went on to win again before his tragically early death. Old Tom survived all his children and such was his standing in the community that when he died in 1908, all the St Andrews courses stood empty on the day of his funeral.

In memory of Allan Robertson – 'Champion Golfer of Scotland'. He is buried at St Andrews.

Perhaps the longest series of challenge matches took place between Old Tom and his arch rival Willie Park. For close on 30 years they played for considerable sums of money on dozens of different courses and, almost inevitably, their final match came to a bizarre end.

Apart from the wealthy golfers who put up the money for the challenge, hundreds of supporters would have invested a few shillings on the outcome, and at Musselburgh in 1882 the local support became a little too active. With Park two up and six to play, the referee stopped play because spectators were interfering with the balls. Old Tom and the referee took advantage of the fact that they were close to Foremen's ale house and retired for a small refreshment while the crowds calmed down.

Winner of the first British Open, Willie Park, 1860. His fourth and last Open win came 15 years later.

The most famous trophy in golf – the silver claret jug presented to every British Open winner since 1872.

Willie Park stayed on the course and when his patience ran out he sent an ultimatum to the inn. 'Come out and finish the match or I'll play the remaining holes and claim the stakes.' Morris chose to have another drink, Park claimed the match, and their long years of rivalry were at an end.

Challenge matches had been the lifeblood of

golf since the game began. When the Duke of York, who was later to become James II of England, was once involved in a bitter dispute with two visiting English noblemen, it was agreed that a golf match should decide the outcome and the Duke chose his partner with great care.

John Pattersone was an Edinburgh shoemaker with a formidable record as a golfer and his contribution to the match ensured that the English were repulsed. The Duke expressed his gratitude in hard currency and although the amount received by Pattersone was not recorded, he used the money to build a house in the centre of Edinburgh. He called the house 'Golfer's Land' and the name plaque bearing the motto 'Far and Sure' can still be seen in the heart of the city.

IT was not really until the advent of the Open Championship in 1860 that stroke-play golf came into being. For hundreds of years competitions had been decided by man-to-man match play – the style of play which proves so popular today in Ryder Cup encounters.

When Prestwick Golf Club members contributed £25 for a leather belt with silver buckles to be offered as the prize in an open competition in 1860, they invited every known golf club to send 'two professional players who must be respectable caddies'. In those days caddies and professionals were one and the same – carrying the clubs for wealthy members one day, partnering them in challenge matches for large sums of money the next.

It was decided that the belt would be awarded for one year to the player with the lowest score over three rounds of the 12-hole course. The response was disappointing, but the club persisted and kept the competition going for the next 10 years, with never more than 17 entries.

The fortunes of the championship were probably saved by the fact that Young Tom Morris won the event three years in a row from 1868. He secured his third victory with the help of an eagle three at the 578-yard first hole. Under the rules of the competition the champion's belt now became his property. There may have been a problem in raising more funds for a new trophy, because there was no championship in 1871.

The silver claret jug which is still awarded

to the new champion was bought jointly by Prestwick, the Royal and Ancient Golf Club of St Andrews and the Honourable Company of Edinburgh Golfers and play resumed at Prestwick in 1872.

From that date the championship alternated between the three host clubs, St Andrews always attracting the largest entry, the numbers increasing to 26 in 1873 and to 46 in 1879. As more and more clubs were formed in Scotland and England the entries increased – and so did the numbers involved in organising the event. A consortium of 26 clubs eventually voted in 1919 to hand over the running of the championship to the Royal and Ancient.

While the proliferation of golf clubs throughout Scotland and England was helping to establish the Open in the game's history as the oldest championship, golf was also spreading its wings much further afield.

Golf was not confined to Scotland, as this poster shows. Arnaud Massy, the club professional, won the British Open in 1907.

It followed two very different routes. Empire builders and traders planted it in places like India, China and America. Wealthy aficionados scattered the seeds on their grand tours through Europe.

The country which took to the game most readily, and has since had the greatest influence over its development, was America. Scotsman John Reid is regarded as the father of American golf. Born in Dunfermline, he had lived in America for many years when, in late 1887, he asked his friend Bob Lockhart to bring back golf clubs and balls on his return from a trip to Scotland. Over three makeshift holes in a meadow opposite his home, he demonstrated the game to his friends on Washington's birthday, 22 February 1888. There was sufficient interest and encouragement from neighbours and friends for him to call a meeting in November of that year and formally establish the St Andrews Golf Club at Yonkers-on-the-Hudson, New York.

Dorset Fields in Vermont and Foxburg Country Club in Pennsylvania claim to have been in existence in 1886 and 1887 respectively, but Reid's portrait hangs in a place of honour in the headquarters of the United States Golf Association at Far Hills, New Jersey.

Strangely enough, there are records of golf having been played a hundred years earlier in the South. The *South Carolina and Georgia Almanac* refers to the formation of a golf club at Charleston in 1786 and there is further evidence of a second club just across the state line at Savannah, Georgia before 1800. But all trace of these clubs disappeared with the start of the Anglo-American war of 1812.

What America had missed over the previous 100 years, however, they rapidly made up for when the game got a second chance in the 1890s, with more than 1000 courses being built by the turn of the century. In 1895 the United States Golf Association was formed and the official versions of the American Amateur and Open Championships were first held in that year, although events for professionals and amateurs had previously been played.

By 1904, Walter Travis had become the first American to win the British Amateur Championship and the golfers from the new world were heading slowly but inexorably towards an extended period of world domination.

A close-up of the flag at the 10th hole in the 1984 US Open shows the crest of the USGA, founded in 1894.

No other country came close to matching the speed of development of the game in America, but little outposts of golf were springing up around the world. In the decades before and after the end of the 19th century, courses were built in Ireland and Wales, France and Portugal, Australia, Canada, Japan and China.

Scots soldiers were never slow to produce a club and a few balls from their kit bags in order to pursue their game wherever they were stationed. Engineers, doctors and merchants were equally keen to lay out primitive courses in the most unlikely and unsuitable places. Inevitably, local youngsters would be recruited as caddies and were soon eager to try the funny foreign game themselves.

Yet the main protagonists would be the expatriate Britons and a few of the wealthiest residents. From being a game for everyone in its early days in Scotland, it had been taken over by the class-conscious Victorians and exported as part of their pickled in aspic, pink gin world. Even when the Victorian era was long gone, expatriates continued to surround themselves with the trappings of their former glories and golf remained an exclusive game.

Australia, Canada and America were young countries with the confidence to shake off the Victorian cobwebs and begin to develop golf along more healthy lines, but in many parts of Europe, Africa and South America the game still has great snob appeal and the rich are not keen to share it with anyone else.

Until the First World War, even the Americans could not explode the image of golf being a rather exclusive, upper-crust pastime, but the rip-roaring attitudes of the 1920s broke down most of the social barriers. The Americans spend a greater proportion of their income on personal enjoyment than any nation on earth, and the free-wheeling, big-spending days of the twenties were largely responsible for this change in attitude as golf got swept along with the tide.

Scotland played a big part in the development of American golf. Literally hundreds of golfers, professionals and talented amateurs, were recruited to help establish new courses and clubs across the Atlantic. No less than 287 from the Carnoustie area of Angus left Scotland's east coast for lucrative appointments with new American clubs.

They often gave advice on the design of the course, helped supervise the construction and became responsible for the greenkeeping, as well as selling golf equipment and giving lessons. Many a new golfer in America's Midwest developed a quick, flat swing because his club professional had grown up on the windswept, hard links at Carnoustie where that was the most effective way to play good golf.

But the American way was destined to be different. There are very few genuine links areas on either the east or west coast of the North American continent and not many parts of the country are exposed to the almost constant winds which create much of the challenge of traditional links golf.

An approach shot to a green guarded by one bunker on the left and grassy hollows to the right can offer a real challenge if the wind is strong from the right or left for 250 days a year. It becomes a boring nonentity if the trees are motionless against a clear sky for nine months out of 12.

If the chosen ground for a new course in America did not have the benefit of the sandhills, gorse and natural bunkers which gave birth to the game on Scotland's east coast, then contours and hazards had to be created. Bunkers, or traps as the Americans soon learned to call them, became the prime weapon in giving courses shape and interest. Sites which included mature trees and natural lakes were hunted out by a growing band of new golf course designers.

Creating new contours by digging out by hand and using horses pulling draglines was a laborious practice, but it was the only way

The practice ground at the 1988 British Open attracts quite a crowd to watch the top players warm up.

designers could transform unpromising tracts of land into some semblance of a Scottish course.

The development of tractors and earth-moving equipment produced a new dimension to course architecture, allowing thousands of cubic yards of earth to be moved and leading directly to the enthusiastic use of water as a hazard on so many American courses. Excavating a series of lakes has three important bearings on a golf

course. They give great visual attraction and form very clear hazards. The earth which is excavated can be used to shape and mound other areas of the course. And the lakes themselves provide reservoirs for watering.

Not only did the shape of courses change in the new world, so did the golf swing. The development of the rubber-cored ball, and later the steel shaft, had an effect on golf throughout the world, but the speed of change and the depth of analysis of the golf swing were unique to America.

Purpose-built golf courses were equipped with large practice grounds, unlike the traditional Scottish courses which were laid out on narrow strips of land next to the sea and where there was no room for practice areas – unless golfers were prepared to walk to the far end of the course. But practice was not considered part of the game in those days. Players went out to enjoy themselves, to win a match and collect a wager over a few drinks.

Americans, approaching the game as a new sport, not one which had evolved as part of their culture over centuries, had the benefit of land and money to create lavish clubhouses with excellent catering facilities and to develop practice areas on which their Scottish professionals would teach them the secrets of the game.

Newly arrived from Scotland and England, the imported professionals walked straight into positions of authority and responsibility. Their advice was asked for on all aspects of the game, they were paid decent salaries and given extensive shops in which they were encouraged to stock all the latest equipment.

It was a far cry from the situation at home where they acted as caddy masters, had no premises in which to sell the clubs they made, and were treated as club servants. At many of the more exclusive clubs in England, the professional was not allowed in the clubhouse until well after the Second World War.

On the other side of the Atlantic at the turn of the century, the professional was the star of the show. He had usually been encouraged to come to the United States by a wealthy member of the club, who delighted in introducing the golfing expert to his circle of friends. From being poorly paid club servants, the immigrants suddenly found themselves mixing in high society. It was no wonder that many took American nationality and settled quickly into their new homeland.

Back in Britain, unrest had been simmering among the caddy-professionals since the 1890s. It flared briefly when the Honourable Company of Edinburgh Golfers moved from Musselburgh to Muirfield and announced their intention of staging the Open Championship for the normal £30 prize fund. The residents of Musselburgh, led by the redoubtable Willie Park, raised £100 for an event to be played on the same day.

In order to keep the Open alive the Honourable Company increased their prize to £110 and the competitors benefited twice – the Musselburgh event being played the following day. Seven years later the Open prize fund had remained static and a group of professionals threatened not to take part in the 1899 event at Sandwich. The senior professionals, led by JH Taylor, Harry Vardon, James Braid and Willie Park, intervened and were able to negotiate a £30 increase.

The legendary JH Taylor, five times winner of the British Open.

It was this incident which brought John Henry Taylor into the limelight. He had already won the Open twice and was to claim victory three more times before the war. He had little formal education, having left school at the age of 11, but he was to become a forceful speaker and a natural leader of his fellow professionals.

Their situation was not enviable. Many worked for small clubs which paid no retainer. In the days when clubs and balls were made by hand, the professionals sold what they made in their own workshops. But they could not compete with the new processes of mass production and a valuable part of their earnings started to slip away.

The wealthier clubs did pay a small retainer but expected their professional to be on hand to make and repair clubs, give lessons, supervise the caddies and maintain the course. The hours were impossibly long and there was never a day off. When clubs started looking at the possibility of selling the mass-produced clubs and balls directly to their members, cutting the professional out of the picture, Taylor felt the time had come for action.

In response to a leading article in *Golf Illustrated* written by its sympathetic editor Harold Hilton, a distinguished amateur who had twice won the Open Championship, a meeting of 50 professionals took place in September 1901 which formed the London and Counties Professional Golfers' Association. The aims of the Association were: 'To promote interest in the game of golf; to protect and advance the mutual and trade interests of all members; to hold meetings and tournaments periodically for the encouragement of the younger members; to act as an agency for assisting any professional or clubmaker to obtain employment.'

The first event organised under their auspices was held at the Tooting Bec Golf Club and the £5 first prize went to JH Taylor himself. The club presented a trophy for the event, which is now awarded annually to the member with the lowest single-round score in the Open Championship.

The formation of the Professional Golfers' Association did much to improve the working conditions and enhance the reputation of the game's experts in Britain, and it has expanded to a present-day membership of some 3500. But it could not begin to match the respect and the lifestyle of the pioneers of American golf in the early days of the 20th century.

America was taking to golf in a big way. Not everyone who wanted to play golf could afford membership of the smartest country clubs, but with 300 public courses created in the 1920s and a host of more affordable clubs springing up on the outskirts of most major cities, the game was essentially open to all-comers.

The relative affluence of the period after the First World War, the Let's-do-it-today-in-case-things-get-worse-again-tomorrow attitude to life, and the mass production of cheap motor cars all conspired to make golf an integral part of the new American way of life. When Bing Crosby sang 'Right Down the Middle' it was only the tip of the iceberg of songs and vaudeville turns which had featured golf since the 'roaring twenties'.

It was clearly a game which reflected the American attitude. Every golfer stands by his own merits. His success does not depend on anyone else. The game is clean-cut and gentlemanly and

Harold Hilton in 1911. The only Englishman ever to win the US Amateur Championship, he also won the British Open twice.

played in the big outdoors. Players don't need to be six feet three and 24 years old to be the best. Man or woman, young or old, anyone can play.

Golf and the aspirational American society were made for each other. Movie stars and politicians played – everyone else wanted to do the same. The game became fashion conscious in the twenties to suit the country club image. And the clubs themselves expanded to cater for wives and families, for entertaining and business meetings, for swimming and tennis.

It became important to dress for golf. Baggy plus-fours in lightweight material and fancy colours, matched with two-tone shoes and a sleeveless Argyll sweater, would be the order of the day, but golfers would change into fashionable blazers to join the ladies for lunch.

In Britain's elite clubs, members would still play in shirt and tie, but would most probably keep an old pair of trousers and a sweater rolled up in their locker for use on the course. It was not until the 1960s that the majority of Britain's golfers thought about dressing up, rather than dressing down, for golf.

Jock Hutchison emigrated to Chicago from his native Scotland. The move did him good – he won the US PGA in 1920 and the Open in 1921.

It was entirely fitting that the man who made the first significant breach in Britain's domination of the championships on both sides of the Atlantic was a larger than life character who embodied all the flamboyant excesses of the American version of the game and allied it to superb skills on the course. Walter Hagen, with sleeked-back hair, black and white shoes and colourful plus-fours – already known as knickers in his home country – won the Open Championship at Sandwich in 1922, sparking a run of 11 American victories in 12 years. Three times the trophy was to bear his name.

Jock Hutchison, who took the title at St Andrews in 1921 after a 36-hole play-off with amateur Roger Wethered, entered the championship as an American citizen from Chicago. But he had been born and brought up in St Andrews before emigrating to America, so Hagen can rightly be regarded as the first native-born American to take the title.

Hagen was always a snappy dresser, loved to socialise, had been known to go straight from an all-night party to the golf course still in his dinner jacket, and played a no-holds-barred game of golf in which playing safe had no part. When told that his opponent for the following day's match had been in bed for hours, Hagen downed his drink and asked: 'Yeah, but is he sleeping?'

Hagen brought a sense of fun and irreverence to the somewhat staid arena of championship golf and gave eloquent warning that although the Scots undoubtedly invented and exported golf, America had successfully re-invented it.

The breach in the wall that Hagen opened soon let in big-hitting Jim Barnes, another exiled Scot Tommy Armour, Gene Sarazen, Densmore Shute and the most remarkable golfer of that or any other age, Bobby Jones. He won the United States Open at the age of 21 and for seven years dominated the game at both amateur and professional level. In his final competitive year of 1930 he won the Open and Amateur Championships of Britain and America in one season – a feat which will never be equalled. He was a qualified lawyer with his own practice, who played the championships during breaks from the office. To the many fine players from the new world could now be added the name of their first superstar.

Out of this era of euphoria, American golf rapidly became a promotional tool, not just for individual businessmen seeking to impress a client but for whole communities. By staging a major tournament a city could attract all sorts of newspaper and radio publicity. A formula was established which enabled an extensive network of events to be staged around the country.

Local businessmen would contribute towards the prize-money as sponsors, suitably rewarded with advertising in the programme and tickets for themselves and their guests. The host club would give its facilities free of charge in return for the publicity value. Members of the club would act as unpaid stewards, marshals and drivers because they wanted their club and their community to do as good a job as possible.

It worked like a dream, and a regular tournament schedule was soon in operation with, by the standards of the day, large amounts of prize-money for the professionals to fight over. In essence, the same method of financing and staging events on the American professional tour is in operation today – the blazer-clad marshals and officials who look so smart on television not only giving up their time and effort for no financial reward, but also having bought their own uniforms.

In this way a regular competitive circuit was established at a very early stage in the development of the game in America, and it was not long before it began to throw up players of the calibre of Sam Snead and Ben Hogan. A constant diet of competitive play, excellent practice facilities and fine courses, not to mention substantial rewards for victory, spurred many thousands of good players to devote hours to practice and analysis of the mechanics of the game.

Where it had been a natural, instinctive game when it left the shores of Scotland, it was now subjected to detailed scrutiny, broken down into thousands of words and hundreds of pictures as players looked for ways to improve their striking of the ball.

Hogan was more dedicated than most, spending literally thousands of hours on the practice ground trying to build a swing which would repeat time and time again under the pressure of tournament play. It took him 15 years of supremely hard work before he won his first championship, but he won two more, and 19 other tournaments, in the following two seasons. Returning from a near-fatal road crash he won the Masters, US Open and British Open in the one season of 1953, but did not compete in the final championship of the year, the US PGA.

Both Jones and Hogan captured the public imagination in a way that few other sportsmen have achieved and they advanced the cause of golf by leaps and bounds. Universities started to establish golf teams and to award scholarships, and it was through this system that Arnold Palmer and Jack Nicklaus emerged to dominate the world of golf in the 1960s and beyond.

It was this college system, leading directly

The legendary Bobby Jones. The world's greatest golfer remained an amateur, achieved the Grand Slam and retired at 28.

into a highly competitive, year-round tournament circuit with vast sums of prize-money, allied to first-class courses and excellent practice facilities, that enabled America to leap ahead of the rest of the world, leaving Britain trailing far in its wake.

But the breakthrough by Tony Jacklin in the Open Championship of 1969 triggered a revival of British fortunes and brought European golfers into the frame for the first time. Such is the strength and competitive nature of the European tour today that each event is worth more than the whole of the 1971 season, and the pendulum of golfing fortune has swung decisively back to the eastern side of the Atlantic.

THE ROYAL & ANCIENT CLUB

FROM within the grey stone walls and tall windows of their headquarters between the 18th green of the Old Course and the North Sea, the Royal and Ancient Golf Club of St Andrews wields a mighty influence around the entire golfing world.

Yet, in reality, it is a private club, with a mere handful of members actually resident in the fine old university city that has become universally known as the home of golf.

Although there is much evidence that golf has been played at St Andrews for well over five

centuries, along the linksland running northwards from the city, the distinction of setting down the first rules of the game belongs not to the Royal and Ancient club but to the Honourable Company of Edinburgh Golfers, while the Open Championship was conceived and run by Prestwick Golf Club for 12 years before the R and A become involved.

The story of St Andrews' rise to pre-eminence starts in the smoke-filled, low-ceilinged back room of the Black Bull Tavern in 1754 when 22 noblemen and gentlemen of the Kingdom of Fife met to form the Society of St Andrews Golfers. They followed the pattern set some 10 years earlier in Edinburgh when the Gentlemen Golfers of Leith had applied to the city council for a silver club to be presented for annual competition, the first time that a formal event had been contemplated. Until that time golf had been delightfully haphazard, with matches arranged for wagers large and small and invariably settled in the local tavern, for no clubhouses existed.

'The auld gray toon' – St Andrews, home of the Royal and Ancient club.

One of the most imposing views in golf – the R and A clubhouse at St Andrews.

Michael Bonallack, Secretary of the R and A.

But from the time that the Gentlemen Golfers of Leith, later to become known as the Honourable Company of Edinburgh Golfers, formed themselves into an official society, other groups, such as those in St Andrews, began to emerge.

Their sole aim was personal enjoyment, grouping together like-minded men to play golf and eat and drink to excess in the local inn when the matches were finished. While the underlying rules of play adopted by each society had much in common, they did differ in detail from one area to another.

Members of these societies continued to take their place with other local golfers on the common links, but those who played at Leith, where there were only five holes, eventually moved to Musselburgh in search of more space.

Finally the Honourable Company bought their own land at Gullane and created the Muirfield course.

The St Andrews golfers were more fortunate, the links area being large enough to accommodate all who wanted to play. In consequence, as the Edinburgh players moved about and lost a certain identity, the St Andrews society grew in strength and became a focal point within the game.

In 1834, King William IV became patron of the St Andrews society and for the first time the official title of Royal and Ancient Golf Club was bestowed. The present clubhouse was built in 1854 at a cost of £800, a sum shared by the Union Club which also occupied the building. In a direct link with those early days, Union Club silver is still in daily use in the R and A dining room.

The other factor which affected the status of St Andrews so strongly was its location. Golf had developed along the eastern coast of Scotland between Edinburgh and Aberdeen and was played inland as far as Perth. St Andrews was the geographical centre. When the western outpost at Prestwick came up with the idea of the Open Championship, few golfers were prepared to make the arduous journey and in the Open's first 12 years the entry was never more than 17, once as low as six.

When Edinburgh and St Andrews were asked to join in the staging of the event after 1872, it was always more heavily supported when held in the town that was to earn its name as the home of golf.

It was almost inevitable that when the leading clubs were seeking a uniform code of rules, they entrusted the R and A with the task. The first Rules of Golf committee was established in 1897 and the R and A are still responsible for administering the rules worldwide, with the exception of the United States and Mexico which come under the umbrella of the United States Golf Association. But there is close liaison between the two bodies and a common set of rules has been in existence for many years.

The Open Championship continued to expand until eventually a consortium of 26 clubs became involved in the event, but a unanimous vote in 1919 handed over the entire organisation of the Open and Amateur championships to the R and A.

Since that time the club has taken on responsibility for the Boys', Youths' and Seniors' championships and the Walker Cup matches against America. The Open has grown into a multi-million pound event for which detailed planning starts at least two years in advance.

Under the leadership of five-times Amateur champion Michael Bonallack, a small team of expert administrators take care of the club's outside activities, with the backing of club committees.

The R and A also gives a strong lead in golf through seminars and conferences covering all aspects of the game, from handicapping systems

At the Open Championship the R and A have hundreds of stewards and observers to monitor the play.

and the possible entry of golf into the Olympics to course design and agronomy. They have also devoted much energy to the provision of new courses.

More concrete help is given through a large number of grants and loans made from the profits generated by the Open Championship. Amateur golfing bodies in Britain and overseas have received help in developing the game, and the Golf Foundation, which works tirelessly for junior golf, has been a major beneficiary. Handicapped golfers and students have received help, and money has been invested in research into greenkeeping methods. Close to £3 million has been donated to these projects in a five-year period.

In the best traditions of British clubs, the business is carried out with a very relaxed, almost casual air. A wonderful sense of irreverent, self-deprecating humour pervades the atmosphere. This is the least stuffy of gentlemen's clubs – firmly planted in the modern world and carrying out many worthwhile tasks, while always remaining true to the traditions of the past.

EQUIPMENT TODAY

MODERN golf equipment is designed and manufactured with scientific precision to provide the performance, power and accuracy which all golfers demand. Highly researched designs and precision manufacturing techniques allow golf clubs to be tailored to the physique, style of play and even the temperament of almost any golfer. New materials and innovations in head and shaft design continue to appear in the quest for clubs which will hit the ball further and with never a hint of a hook or a slice.

The result is that the golfer of the 1990s is faced with an almost bewildering choice of materials and designs when selecting a new set of clubs.

It is all a far cry from the earliest days of golf when woods were roughly hewn pieces of hedgethorn or briar and irons were forgings of the most basic kind.

Since the golfer's only contact with the ball is through the club, it is obvious that its design, balance and swing characteristics should be right for him if he is to enjoy any success at all.

In recent years golfers have become aware of the need to have clubs which 'fit' them comfortably, like a pair of good shoes, and are increasingly taking advantage of the custom-made services offered by the major manufacturers.

Having been 'measured' by his professional, the golfer can be certain that his new clubs will have the correct swing weight, loft and lie; that the shaft material and the degree of flex will be the best for his game, taking age and physical strength into consideration; and even that the grips will be of the best thickness in relation to the size of his hands.

When built into a set of clubs correctly, these elements can help the golfer improve his game significantly.

Although scientists and technicians play important roles in developing and manufacturing modern golf clubs, the skilled craftsman club-maker is still much in demand and retains the respect enjoyed by his predecessors in the 18th and 19th centuries.

Hand crafting woods for drivers.

This was the so-called 'Golden Age' of clubmaking, when every club was hand made and bore the character of the man who crafted it. Clubs took a long time to make and were expensive, and so the number of people who could afford to play golf was limited.

Originally, most golf club heads were made from hedgethorn which was grown at a sloping angle to make shaping them easier. Hedgethorn survived until the gutta percha ball replaced the featherie. Whippy shafts, usually made from ash, were best for use with the featherie ball but the 'guttie' demanded something much stiffer and gradually hickory became the favoured wood.

Later, the introduction from the USA of the softer, rubber-cored golf ball led to the use of an American hardwood called persimmon for making heads; and despite the advanced technology of the late 20th century persimmon woods are still very popular.

Persimmon is a very slow-growing wood and is therefore expensive. It is, however, extremely dense which means it transmits a high proportion of the power generated in the swing to the ball and gives excellent distance. It is also a most beautiful wood and when fashioned by a craftsman its grain and lustre make a persimmon-headed club a joy to own and look at as well as a pleasure to use.

Metal-headed woods came to the fore in the 1980s with the development of precise casting techniques which enabled finely-balanced heads with walls of the correct thickness to be produced on a consistent basis. Metal woods are hollow – though most are filled with an impact absorbing foam – and this allows the weight to be distributed around the head for optimum power and balance. This is known as peripheral weighting and has the benefit of creating a larger hitting area on the clubface, so that slightly off-centre hits produce a better result than with a conventional club.

Metal woods can also be made lighter than wooden clubs and this allows the golfer to generate greater clubhead speed and distance – something which is further enhanced by the need for less loft on the clubface.

Carbon graphite – which can be injection or compression moulded – and ceramics are other materials which are used with success in the

A mobile workshop travels around with the European Tour, carrying out instant repairs for the top players.

Master clubmaker Harry Busson creating another masterpiece.

manufacturer of 'woods'. Graphite in particular has won many adherents because of its lightness, density and strength which together can produce outstanding power. Manufacturing techniques also allow weight distribution to be finely controlled. The lightness of graphite also allows larger than standard heads to be produced without incurring a weight penalty. This provides more power and can also enhance the player's confidence.

In the early days of golf there were only wooden clubs. The featherie ball did not demand iron clubs and even if they had been necessary it is doubtful if the techniques existed to produce them with any consistent quality. The featherie ball would have been quickly ruined by strikes from roughly forged irons – and balls were just as expensive to replace as clubs.

So it was not until the introduction of the solid gutta percha ball in 1848 that irons became part of the golfer's armoury. The earliest irons were hand-forged and their varied designs were a tribute to the clubmakers' ingenuity. Names like rut niblick, water iron and sand rake give a clue to their individual purpose. The numbering of irons is a relatively recent development and well into the 1960s it was commonplace to hear golfers referring to mashie niblicks and cleeks.

As the working of metal became more sophisticated, so the clubmakers evolved the basic blade shape for irons, which remains virtually unchanged. Various patterns were etched, punched or scored onto the faces of these early clubs in an attempt to give more control and a better strike. Today's grooves are the result and their function is to impart backspin to the ball to make it fly higher and stop more quickly when landing on the green.

Modern irons are either forged or cast, usually from stainless steel, although copper, beryllium and other alloys are also used. Forged irons give a slightly softer feel and are favoured by good players who demand maximum control. The traditional, simple blade design with a narrow sole is also the choice of most accomplished golfers since it rewards those who strike the ball precisely and consistently.

For most amateurs, however, the development of 'heel and toe' irons has been the key to better scoring and more enjoyable golf. These clubs have their weight distributed between the heel and the toe, a feature which gives excellent balance and creates a larger hitting area or 'sweetspot'. Thus, a ball hit towards the toe or heel of the club will usually result in the ball deviating from its line to a lesser degree than would be the case with blade clubs.

Golf balls through the ages – from the featherie through the guttie and the early rubber-cored balls to the highly developed ball of the 1990s.

Heel and toe irons also have a broader sole than is found on blade clubs and this makes them much easier to play from both the fairway and the semi-rough. They help the player get the ball into the air, are more forgiving of mis-hits and consequently give the player confidence.

Several manufacturers also produce graphite-headed irons which are claimed to offer the same benefits as graphite woods – but at a price.

More realistically, graphite is now accepted as being at the forefront of shaft technology and, together with even more exotic materials like boron and titanium, is almost as popular as stainless steel. Stainless steel shafts were introduced in America in the 1930s and were quickly adopted by leading players like Byron Nelson who appreciated their high performance compared with hickory shafts.

Shaft manufacture is a science in its own right but suffice to say that swing weights, frequency matching, flex ratings and kick-points are all painstakingly co-ordinated to give the golfer the optimum blend of power and control to suit his game, regardless of the material he selects.

Some modern drivers using the latest in technology and materials. An interesting comparison with those pictured on page 15.

The bag room at a European Tour event, with a valuable collection of personalised equipment.

Older players and ladies will usually benefit from high-flexing or whippy shafts which will help them generate more clubhead speed and distance. Conversely, strong amateurs and professionals need stiff shafts to harness their power. They generate sufficient clubhead speed with their swing and look to the stiffness of the shaft to give them accuracy to complement distance.

Gone, then, are the days when after playing a game the golfer would stand his hickory shafted clubs in a bucket of water to keep them supple and prevent them from warping.

Rapid development of golf ball technology has been a major influence on the growth of the game. Today's golf balls are high-tech products – and there has never been a wider choice.

There are four main types of golf ball available today and their differing constructions result in different playing characteristics (see

Golfers nowadays have wooden tees, ball markers, pitch-mark repair forks and printed scorecards.

For the club player, probably the biggest advance in golf ball technology was the introduction in the 1970s of the two-piece ball. With its large polybutadiene core and virtually cut-proof cover, it provided greater distance and outstanding durability – qualities close to most golfers' hearts.

Because golf balls must comply with the distance and velocity regulations specified by the Royal and Ancient Golf Club of St Andrews and the United States Golf Association, manufacturers are turning their attention increasingly to improved aerodynamics to produce balls which fly further and which are ever more accurate.

Dimple patterns are devised using computer-aided design techniques with myriad combinations of dimple size, depth and edge-sharpness being assessed before prototype balls are made. The use of computers has certainly speeded up golf ball development as scientists seek to produce dimple patterns with the highest possible degree of symmetry. Symmetry in the dimple lay-out produces consistency in flight, while it is also important that as much of the ball's surface as possible is covered by dimples.

Prototype balls are tested under all conditions by all types of golfers – from tournament professionals to club handicappers. Some companies, like Dunlop, also use specially designed flight test machines which can produce the perfect swing with any club, thus giving technologists a consistent base of measurement against which all golf balls can be assessed.

The flight test machine provides a bank of data on spin rates, elevation, carry and total

overleaf). Thus most players can find a ball to suit their style of play. However, all of them represent a quantum leap in product development since the early days of golf.

Over the years liquid centres have replaced the original solid cores, although both are still in use today, and manufacturers have developed new compounds of synthetic materials to give the golf ball improved velocity and distance, something which is now strictly controlled by golf's governing bodies.

Testing out the modern golf ball washer.

distance, all of which is analysed by computer. This information, together with measurements of windspeed and direction, humidity and temperature, allows the manufacturers to see quickly exactly how their new dimple patterns and rubber compounds will perform in practice.

It is probably a good thing that the R and A and the USGA demand that all golf equipment conforms to their rules (clubs are also covered). For it is not impossible to imagine equipment manufacturers, given an entirely free hand, producing clubs and balls which would reduce the longest holes to a drive and a pitch.

That would render most of our courses obsolete and change the essential nature of the game. However, refinement and development by degrees will enable people to play and enjoy the

game even more, with clubs that are easier to swing and more forgiving, and balls which are more stable in flight and thus more accurate.

All that will then be required for a single figure handicap will be the human element. And that is one essential part of the golfing story which has not changed over the years.

The Modern Golf Ball

One-Piece Ball

The simplest type of ball to manufacture and the least effective in performance. Compression-moulded from a plug of rubber, this is a cheap ball which is often used on driving ranges etc.

Two-Piece Ball

Comprises an inner core of about 1½ inches in diameter made from a resilient polybutadiene material, and a compression or injection moulded cover. An extremely effective type of golf ball – hard, long lasting and giving excellent distance. However, the two-piece ball's hardness can make it 'lively' for chipping and putting, but most amateurs find this an acceptable trade-off for the extra distance.

Three-Piece (or thread-wound) Ball

A small rubber sphere is surrounded by tightly wound elastic thread to give high compression and resilience, and then given a tough Surlyn cover, similar to that of a two-piece ball. The three-piece construction gives slightly less distance than a two-piece but it does take more backspin and is thereby easier to control around the greens.

Balata Ball

Construction is similar to the three-piece ball except that the centre is usually a hollow rubber sphere filled with clay paste and water. The centre is then frozen before being wrapped in elastic thread. The cover is processed natural balata which is also vulcanised.

The balata cover is very soft compared with Surlyn and, with the liquid centre, gives optimum spin, feel and control. Professionals invariably use balata balls since a slight loss of distance is irrelevant compared with the ability it gives them to shape their shots and exercise a high degree of control.

Balata balls are easily damaged by mis-hits. They are also expensive and are therefore little used by the average amateur.

This flight test machine produces a perfect swing every single time and is used to assess the performance of new golf balls and clubs.

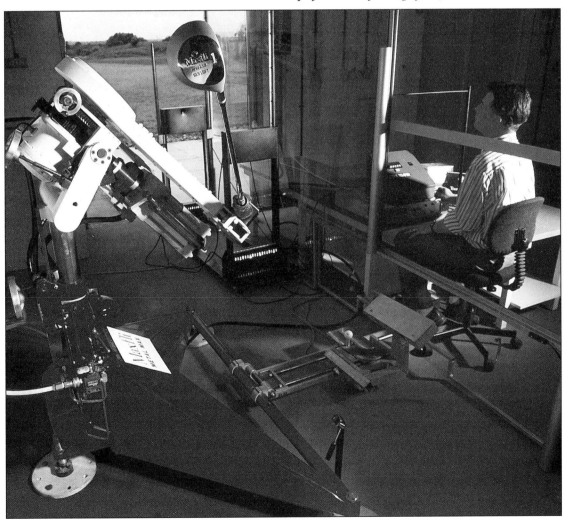

GOLF & ROYALTY

ROYAL involvement with golf has been good news and bad news from the earliest moments of the game. James II of Scotland outlawed golf because it prevented the ordinary citizens from regular practice with the bow and arrow, which he felt was more important in 1457 when his realm was under threat from the English.

There is no evidence that he ever played the game himself, but James IV, although he too banned golf in 1491, was known to enjoy a round or two. It is not known if he broke his own edict while his citizens were busy pulling their bow strings, but as soon as the act outlawing the game was repealed in 1503, as a result of his marriage to Henry VII's daughter, items began to appear in the accounts of the Lord High Treasurer which proved that he was again actively involved.

On February 4 of that year the following appears: 'Item – to golf clubbes and ballis to the King.' Other entries over the following years show the purchase of more clubs and balls and the handing over of a sum of money to settle a golfing debt with the Earl of Bothwell.

James V played regularly over the private course of the Earl of Wemyss in East Lothian and his daughter, Mary, Queen of Scots, was proficient at the game, playing often in St Andrews and elsewhere.

When her son James VI became the first monarch to rule south of the border as well, as James I of England, he took his clubs with him and soon had both his sons playing in the London area, giving rise to the claim that Royal Blackheath was the first golf club, founded in 1608. In fact, as we have seen, there is no evidence that the club existed before the 1770s.

His surviving son, who became Charles I of England, adopted the Francis Drake technique when interrupted during a round at Leith to be told of the Irish rebellion. He finished his game before attempting to tackle the crisis.

Both Charles II and his brother James II

Prince Rainier of Monaco, a keen golfer, with Gary Player.

HRH Prince Andrew at the British Open, Royal Birkdale, 1991. He is the only member of the British royal family with an interest in the sport.

were also keen and regular golfers, but with the disappearance of the Stuarts from the line of descent there is no further mention of royal golf until William IV created the first Royal golf club by granting Perth Golfing Society the right to use the Royal prefix in 1833. The following year he became patron of the Society of St Andrews Golfers and allowed them to change their title to the Royal and Ancient Golf Club of St Andrews. Members still play annually for the medal he presented in 1837 and also for the Queen Adelaide medal which his widow gave to the club when she became patron.

Queen Victoria was not known ever to have played the game, but she agreed to become patron of the R and A and her son became the club captain in 1863 when he was Prince of Wales. He was able to pursue his golfing ambitions by having a course laid out at Windsor.

Golf then missed a royal generation, but George V's three sons were all captains of the R and A between 1922 and 1937. The best golfer of the lot was Edward VIII, who spent less than a year on the throne before he abdicated to marry Mrs Simpson. He often escaped to the golf course during the abdication crisis. He won many competitions, had two holes in one and followed British golf closely from his home near Paris. When Tony Jacklin became the first home player to win the Open for 18 years with his victory at Royal Lytham in 1969, he received a hand-written note of congratulations from the exiled Duke.

His brother George VI did not play regularly, but arrived at Muirfield in time to see Henry Cotton win the 1948 Open. No present member of the British royal family shows any active interest in golf, but in Europe and elsewhere there have been, and still are, many proficient royal golfers.

King Albert of Belgium was involved in the founding of the Royal Golf Club de Belgique in 1906 and King Leopold played in the Belgian Amateur Championship of 1939, the first time a reigning monarch had played in a national championship.

He was one of the best royal golfers of all time, also playing in the French Amateur in 1949. His son, King Baudouin, inherited his father's ability at the game and his love of competition, and he represented his country in the triangular match against France and Holland in 1958. He also partnered Dai Rees in the Gleneagles Hotel pro–am tournament in 1959 – hiding his royal light under the pseudonym Mr B de Rethy. Royal successes, however, are few and far between, perhaps the most noteworthy being that by Prince Claus of the Netherlands who partnered Peter Oosterhuis to victory in the 1974 Dutch Open pro–am.

The Shah of Iran had commissioned the building of several golf courses before he was

King Hassan of Morocco had the beautiful Royal Dar-es-Salaam course built.

overthrown by the revolution, but the Aga Khan was more successful with the magnificent Pevero course which is the centre-piece of his Costa Smeralda project in Sardinia.

Prince Rainier of Monaco is one of Europe's keenest royal players and has played the Old Course at St Andrews, but without question King Hassan of Morocco is currently the world's greatest royal golf enthusiast. He has had two magnificent courses built and plays host annually to a major event to which the world's leading professionals are invited. His guests were rudely interrupted on one occasion when an attempted coup swept through the palace grounds and several professionals were rounded up by armed men. The situation was quickly restored, but one British player was slightly injured. United States Open winner Billy Casper was retained for many years as personal golf instructor to King Hassan.

The game has had royal patronage and support since its very beginnings and many royal golfers have followed the early traditions of the game. It became established that each club captain would mark his year of office by adding a silver ball to the captain's silver club. Royal holders of the office added balls made of gold.

Yet when one venerable Scottish club had their trophies professionally cleaned in time for a significant anniversary, they discovered beneath a gilt covering that all that glistens is truly not gold.

Edward VIII – here as Prince of Wales – was a fine golfer, though after his abdication he played rather less.

WOMEN'S GOLF

WHILST golf has often been thought of as a male preserve, the history of women in golf and their influence in the sport goes back many years.

Mary, Queen of Scots was, we are told, an avid golfer and was seen playing in the fields outside Seton Castle in 1567 shortly after the murder of her philandering husband Lord Darnley – possibly the first-ever reference to a golf widow.

That such a personage should have taken up the game points to its popularity north of the border in those distant times. Certainly it is in Scotland that the next references to the fair sex in golf are found.

The lady members of the Royal Musselburgh Golf Club were obviously keen players, for by 1774 an annual tournament was in place between the married and unmarried ladies, the prize being a fine silver trophy presented by a Mr Thomas McMillan of Shorthope.

Kathy Whitworth – a superb putter who won most of her tournaments on the greens. She was eight times the leading money-winner on tour.

It is not, however, until the late 19th century that one comes across regular mentions of the ladies. In 1867 the St Andrews Ladies' Golf Club was formed; similar ladies' clubs followed at Westward Ho!, North Devon, Musselburgh, Wimbledon and Carnoustie.

The ladies tended to play over shorter courses than the men, some of them being no longer than a pitch and putt course. With hats, high, stiff collars and long, voluminous skirts, swinging a golf club would have been rather more difficult than for the gentlemen.

By 1893, under the guidance of Miss Issette Pearson, later to become Mrs TH Miller, the Ladies' Golf Union was formed. Initially it comprised only 12 clubs but was continually expanded to include clubs from all over the country and the Commonwealth.

Miss Pearson was a member of the Royal Wimbledon Golf Club and it was that club which first decided to hold the British Ladies' Open Championship. By a strange coincidence, at the same time the ladies of Lytham and St Annes advertised in *Golf* magazine that they were to hold an open competition, the prize being a 50-guinea trophy.

On learning of each other's plans the two sets of ladies joined forces to hold the first British Ladies' Open Amateur Championship under the auspices of the LGU. It was played for at St Annes Old Links over a nine-hole course, the ladies going round twice to complete a 4264 yard total, the longest hole being 337 yards.

Thirty-eight ladies competed, the winner being Lady Margaret Scott who went on to win the following two years as well. In the first two finals she beat Miss Pearson, who never won the championship herself. Rather strangely, although players from Ireland and France joined the English ladies, no Scots players made the journey south. They never joined in until 1897, the year that saw two sisters competing the final, the Misses Orr.

Sisters again fought out the final in 1907

Pat Bradley, another American star of the modern era.

*Inter-war golf fashion modelled by Maureen
Orcutt, winner of over sixty amateur titles.*

1908, winning through to the semi-final. Six years later she won it, taking the French and English championships as well. After the War she continued her winning ways with the British Open in both 1920 and 1921, beating the famed Joyce Wethered 4 and 3 at Turnberry. She beat her again that year, too, in the French Open, the only woman ever to have beaten Wethered twice.

The result was reversed the following year at Sandwich, Miss Wethered winning 9 and 7. Their battles continued. Joyce Wethered had almost the last say in 1925 at Troon, the match going to the 37th hole, but that match is supposed to have taken so much out of her that she did not compete the following year, leaving the field open for Miss Leitch's fourth victory. Miss Wethered matched that total in 1929 before going on to marry Lord Heathcoat-Amory, virtually retiring from competitive golf to create one of England's finest country house gardens in Devon.

when May Hezlet beat her sister Florence. It was May's third and final title. Another Hezlet sister, Violet, was runner-up in 1911. Their father, Major Hezlet, had been one of the great amateur golfers of his day and went on to play several matches against Bobby Jones through the 1920s.

By the time the championship final had been extended to 36 holes in 1913, a few dominant figures in the world of ladies' golf had emerged including Dorothy Campbell, whose victory over Violet Hezlet in 1909 brought her the distinction of being the first woman to hold both the British and American Open championship titles in the same year. Lottie Dod, too, having won the Ladies' tennis final at Wimbledon in 1887, turned her attention to golf and became British Ladies' Champion in 1904.

In the last few years before the Great War, another group of golfing sisters emerged, this time the Leitch family from Silloth on the wild Cumbrian coast looking across the Solway Firth towards Scotland, site of one of the most testing links courses in England. Dominant among them was Cecil, who first entered the British Open in

*Mickey Wright, one of America's best ever lady
golfers. She won 81 titles in a 13-year career.*

Louise Suggs, US Open champion in both 1949 and 1952.

South Africa's Sally Little combines power with glamour.

Australian Jan Stephenson, regarded as one of the most exciting players in the women's game. Her career was threatened by a knife attack in Miami in 1990.

By this time ladies' golf was no longer the sole preserve of the English and Scots. Two French ladies, Mlle. Thione de la Chaume (later to become Madame Lacoste) and Mlle. Nanette le Blan, won in 1927 and 1928 respectively and the following year at St Andrews saw the four-times American champion Glenna Collett entering.

Sadly for her, she came up against Joyce Wethered in the final and lost out 3 and 1. She returned the year after, having added a fifth US title, but again was unsuccessful, being beaten by England's 19-year-old Diana Fishwick. Diana, marrying later, became the mother of golf commentator Bruce Critchley.

Yet American golfers had all the while been growing in stature. In 1905 two American sisters, Harriet and Margaret Curtis, had played in the British Open at Cromer in Norfolk and had so

enjoyed the experience that they decided to inaugurate a series of international matches for the ladies.

It took some time to get going but the Curtis Cup, first played for in 1932, is still going strong today. Then, as now, the Americans dominated the event, yet the British Ladies' Open remained the one championship few Americans could actually win, rather an interesting reversal of the situation with the men's US Open.

It was not until 1947 that an American lady first clinched the title. She had been born Mildred Didrikson and had been an avid sportswoman, winning Olympic gold medals in 1932 for javelin and hurdles, as well as setting a new world record in the high jump. She had earlier set four world records at the US National Athletics Championships.

It was at the time of those Olympics in Los Angeles that she first took up golf. Her strength and agility helped her to hit the ball a long way and eventually she learnt the art of shot-making. In the meantime she had married an immigrant Greek wrestler, changing her name to 'Babe' Zaharias, which is the one we remember her by.

In the six rounds of the 1947 British Open she lost only four holes, romping home 5 and 4 in the final. She went on to become a professional, winning 31 titles in 128 starts over an eight-year period, three of them in the US Women's Open. Sadly, she fell victim to cancer and died in 1956.

'Babe' was instrumental in starting the US Ladies' Professional Golf Association in 1950, with several other professionals including Patty Berg. Berg was perhaps the first American golfing 'star' after Glenna Collett, whom she had played in her first ever US Championship final in 1935. Berg was 17; Collett, ironically playing her last final, was 38 and won comfortably, 3 and 2.

Berg was not to win that championship until 1946, three years after turning professional, but had meanwhile ruled the roost in American golf, winning the 1938 Ladies' Amateur, the Title-holders' in 1937, 1938 and 1939 (she was to win four more through to 1957), and the first of seven Western Opens in 1941. She was the leading

Left: *Nancy Lopez brought a touch of star quality to women's golf.*

England's Laura Davies with the US Open trophy, 1989.

Davies packs power into her classy swing.

money-winner in 1954, 1956 and 1957, and in 1952 set a record low score of 64 in Richmond, California which stood for over a decade. It was a remarkable achievement which has guaranteed her place in the hall of fame. Despite a car accident which resulted in a leg bone having to be broken and re-set three times, and operations for cancer, Patty Berg maintained her interest in golf well into the 1970s, particularly helping the causes of children's golf as well as doing all she could to help cancer research.

Despite Berg and a few other ladies turning professional (Berg signed up a sponsorship deal with Wilson to guarantee her an income) there was little prize money for the ladies in those days. Sponsorship receipts, exhibition matches and teaching did, however, secure the select few a reasonable living.

By contrast, in Britain professional golf for ladies was virtually unknown. That was not to change for several years until Colgate sponsored the first ever European Ladies' Open at Sunningdale in 1974. Colgate by then had put a lot of money into the American Tour for the ladies and it was primarily that company's support which set the ladies' circuit in Europe on a surer footing.

Back in the United States, though, ladies' professional golf was going from strength to strength. Patty Berg had bridged the generation gap between the 1930s and 1950s, from Collett to the next great American, Mary Kathryn 'Mickey' Wright in the 1950s.

Born in San Diego, Mickey Wright had a short amateur career before going on to become the most successful lady professional golfer in the US. Between 1961 and 1964 she set records with 44 tournament victories, 13 of them in one season alone. In her career from 1956 to 1969 she won 81 times, adding a final victory in 1973. Her best year saw her winning $36 000. Yet all this time she suffered ill health, with arthritis in her wrists, bad feet and an adverse reaction to the sun. Unlike some in the superstar category she was always a quiet, reserved person, never one to willingly seek media interviews or self-promotion opportunities.

After Wright two other ladies burst onto the scene: Kathy Whitworth, a tall Texan who went on to surpass Wright's 82 career wins (though over a longer period), and Nancy Lopez. Whitworth

was a superb putter who won most of her tournaments on the greens, earning over $900 000 – she was the leading money-winner in no less than eight seasons on tour.

Lopez was born in Torrance (a good golfing name!), California in 1957. By the time she was 20 she had turned professional, having first played for the 1976 American Curtis Cup team. In her first full year on tour she won nine tournaments, five of them consecutively, was the leading money-winner with $190 000 and won the Vare Trophy for the lowest scoring average of 71.76, and the LPGA Championship. Her style and appearance did far more than that, tripling the gates at the tournaments she entered. Here at last was a crowd-puller.

Her second full year was no less successful, with eight victories helping to push her to the top of the money list again, this time with just under $200 000. From then on her victories grew smaller in number, primarily because she had opened the floodgates to good American lady golfers. Now everyone wanted to beat her, raising their games whenever she took part in a tournament. It was to greatly enhance golfing standards, but more importantly helped bring extra money and interest into the Ladies' Tour.

Sponsors now became even more eager to add their names to tournaments, with a consequent rise in media coverage which in turn stimulated more public interest. Many of the players appeared in TV adverts for various products, not all of them associated with golf. And unmistakeably, a certain glamour came into the ladies' game.

Nancy Lopez was attractive and had a winning smile; she was joined by Pat Bradley, Australian Jan Stephenson and South Africa's Sally Little, all of them very attractive on and off the course. Whilst their forerunners had been good golfers, these newcomers swept aside the rather dowdy image of ladies' golf, replacing it with the immaculate grooming of modern superstars.

Glamour also helped to promote products as well. One of the 'products' they were promoting was their own Tour, now run by a full-time Director with a staff to organise the tournament circus as it wound its way round the country. The revitalised interest in the ladies' game saw the winnings on offer rise substantially from about $3 million in 1977 to $6 million in 1981.

Lopez and the others travelled the world, rather than just winning at home. She won the Colgate European Open in both 1978 and 1979. Those victories and the heightened media awareness helped pull British golf out of the doldrums, too.

Carlsberg decided to sponsor a series of 12 events, each with a total purse of £3000. That was the stimulus needed to persuade 17 Britons to turn professional. By the time the first of these events was played, in April 1979 at Tyrells Wood in Surrey, their number had grown to 30 and total prize money for the year was £80000.

Initially there were 18 tournaments and 16 pro–ams; by the end of the year 47 women had joined the Women's Professional Golf Association, putting women's professional golf on the map in Britain and Europe.

Whilst the sums involved fell way short of those on the American circuit, it was a substantial improvement for the ladies to actually get paid for playing golf – they could also find sponsors in the same way as their male counterparts in Europe.

At the end of the first year, Alison Sheard was the leading money-winner with just under £5000 but Cathy Panton was declared Leader of the Order of Merit based on a system of points, weighted for the importance of each event. Several calls have been made for the men's circuit to be judged on the same basis, particularly as Ryder Cup places are at stake in certain years.

By 1980 the Tour had expanded into mainland Europe and the purse had grown to £110 000, spread over 21 events. Hitachi and Volvo joined Carlsberg as sponsors of the Tour. Three years later total prize money had grown to almost £350 000.

European golf was, though, still searching for a superstar to push ladies' golf through the next barrier. In 1985 it got it in the form of Laura Davies, a 21-year-old from Surrey.

Her prodigious power was unique, enabling her to out-drive all opponents, amass £21 736 and top the Order of Merit in her first year. Like Nancy Lopez in the States, she proved this was no flash in the pan by repeating the performance the following year, too.

In 1987 she toured America and won the US

Joe Flanagan who led the WPGET through the difficult 1980s before his retirement in 1991.

Women's Open, becoming only the second Briton to hold both the British and the US title in the same year. Pam Barton, who was killed during the Second World War, had until then been the only player to achieve this double.

In recent years the Ladies' Tour has grown to a total purse of £1.5 million and has produced some startling new stars, including Belgium's Florence Descampe, who at 19 became the youngest winner on tour; Spain's Xonia Wuntsch; Sweden's Liselotte Neumann, who won the 1988 American Open; France's Marie Laure de Lorenzi, who became the leading money winner with close to £100 000 in 1988; and another Swede, Helen Alfredsson, who had her debut victory in the 1990 British Open.

After the retirement of Tour Director Joe Flanagan in 1991, the WPGET (Women's Professional Golf European Tour) appointed a woman, Andrea Doyle, as his successor. With over £2 million in prize money and over 250 members, the European Women's Tour looks set to continue its growth and popularity.

PART TWO:
THE PLAYERS

THE GREATS: PAST & PRESENT

Golden Oldies

Old Tom Morris and Young Tom Morris

It is almost impossible to separate the lives of the two Tom Morrises, as their impact on golf has not decreased over the years.

Old Tom was born in St Andrews on 16 June 1821. At the age of 18 he was apprenticed to Allan Robertson, himself a famous golfer of that age as well as a master clubmaker. The pair made an unbeatable team in any foursome, never losing a match when they played together, often for stakes as high as £200, a vast sum in the mid-19th century.

Sadly they quarrelled in about 1850, due, it seems, to Morris's insistence that they should stop making featherie balls and move on to the longer lasting 'guttie'. Robertson did not agree and the two men parted company, Morris moving to Prestwick in 1851 shortly after the birth of his son, Young Tom.

The Open championship was instituted in 1860 and won by Willie Park. Old Tom came second. The next year, though, he won it, and did so again in 1862, 1864 and 1867. In that year his son, Young Tom, a sprightly 16-year-old, was behind him by four strokes. By then the family had moved back to St Andrews and Young Tom had become something of a prodigy, rather as was Bobby Jones many years later.

In 1868 Young Tom won the Open himself, beating his father and eight other entrants at Prestwick, home of the first 12 Opens. When 1869 and 1870 saw him also victorious, it led to a problem, for the organisers had stipulated that if any golfer won the championship three times he was to keep the fine morocco belt that was presented to the winner. Young Tom, having won it three times, took them at their word and kept it, leaving the organisers with no prize.

There was, therefore, no competition in 1871. The following year, however, a silver claret jug had been put up – to be held only for the year. Young Tom won that, too.

Father and son were by then playing together as a formidable team, and many exhibition matches were played throughout Scotland, often against Willie and Mungo Park of Musselburgh. It was during one such match, at North Berwick in the early autumn of 1875, that tragedy struck. A telegram arrived intimating that Young Tom's wife, having just given birth to their first child, was seriously ill with post-natal complications. The telegram was not handed to Young Tom until he came off the last green, by which time a yacht had been procured to take him back across the Forth to St Andrews. Before he had reached home his wife had died.

He never recovered from the shock and played little golf for the remainder of that year. Living with his father and mother in St Andrews, he went to bed on Christmas Eve that same year. In the morning Old Tom went upstairs to call his son down for Christmas breakfast. There was no reply. Young Tom had died in the night. He was 24.

Old Tom continued playing golf, with a heavy heart, contesting every Open championship up to 1896, when Harry Vardon won his first title. Old Tom was then just over 75 years old and could still swing a club, though by all accounts his putting touch – never that good – had totally deserted him.

He also laid out many golf courses, being one of the first golf architects; many courses today bear his imprint, Carnoustie, Lahinch, Royal Dornoch and Royal North Devon, Nairn and Royal County Down among them.

In 1908, after a fall at the New Club, just off

the 18th fairway at St Andrews close to Granny Clark's Wynd, he died. The 18th at St Andrews is named after him.

Old Tom Morris, 1821–1908. The father of British golf.

JH Taylor

John Henry Taylor – always known as 'JH' – was born in Northam, North Devon, not far from the Royal North Devon Golf Club at Westward Ho!, on 19 March 1871. Growing up near the club he took up golf early, first caddying for the members but then, inevitably, playing himself.

By the time he was 20 he had played, and beaten, many of the leading golfers of the day. He had also become a professional-greenkeeper first at Burnham then Winchester.

In 1893 he entered his first Open championship, held that year at Prestwick, and scored a leading 75 on the first day. Although he fell away to finish 10th overall, that 75 was unbeaten.

The following year the event was held in England for the first time, at Sandwich on the Kent coast. JH won by five clear strokes, driving the ball low and straight and rarely failing to get close on any approach, which he played with a club similar to today's wedges, the first man to do so. Other players tended to run the ball up low.

In 1895 he won again, at St Andrews, leading the field by four strokes. He went on to win the Open a further three times, in 1900, 1909 and 1913, with the 1900 victory at St Andrews again (a course he never liked) being perhaps the sweetest, with an eight-stroke lead over runner-up Harry Vardon and 13 ahead of James Braid in third place.

JH was second himself in 1896 (after a play-off with Vardon), 1904, 1905, 1906 and 1914, as he was the only time he played the US Open, in 1900. He did, though, win the French Open in 1908 and 1909, the German Open in 1912, and the Matchplay Championship in 1908.

He also represented England many times in the annual matches against Scotland, and played for the British team in the first Britain vs America match in 1921 – the series of matches which eventually went on to become the Ryder Cup. He was to captain the winning Ryder Cup team in 1933.

On retiring from playing golf professionally he made the most of his contacts and experience, setting up a club manufacturing business, designing golf courses and writing his autobiography before retiring back home to Northam. He died in February 1963, just a month short of his 92nd birthday.

Harry Vardon

Harry Vardon was born in 1870 in a small cottage in Grouville Bay, in the Channel Island of Jersey. Although the cottage is no longer there, a plaque marks the spot, halfway down what is now the 13th fairway of the Royal Jersey Golf Club.

Harry's elder brother played golf and although Harry himself preferred cricket he was persuaded to become the greenkeeper of Ripon Golf Club in Yorkshire when he was 20, more for his gardening skills than his prowess with a club. Of course his golf improved whilst at Ripon, then at Ganton where he moved in 1895.

He entered his first Open in 1893 and the following year he performed well at Sandwich, coming fifth. A year later he dropped to ninth but 1896 saw him play superbly at Muirfield, where JH Taylor was going for a hat-trick of wins. At the start of the last day Vardon was six behind Taylor, but made up three strokes on the morning round, golfers then playing 36 holes per day. In the afternoon Vardon made up the other three to tie the lead; the two returned the following day to fight it out over a further 36 holes. Vardon won by four.

Thus began a remarkable reign. Although he missed out the following year, he won the Open again in 1898 and 1899 before setting out on a sponsored tour of the United States in 1900. The journey tired him more than he thought, as he travelled 26000 miles to play exhibition matches and promote a golf ball. He did, however, find time to win the US Open in Chicago before returning home exhausted and suffering from what was later diagnosed as tuberculosis.

Nevertheless he added a fourth British Open title in 1903 despite feeling so tired that he felt he would not finish the course. Shortly afterwards he entered a sanatorium, the first of several extended periods of convalescence.

The illness took its inevitable toll and it was not until 1911 that he felt strong enough to beat off the other 225 entrants to win at Sandwich,

Four legends of golf. Standing, left to right: Sandy Herd and JH Taylor. Seated: James Braid and Harry Vardon.

equalling Braid's record of five Open titles set the year before. Two years later Vardon was back in the United States, coming second in the US Open. In the summer of 1914, when war was breaking out in southern Europe, Vardon won at Prestwick, his sixth title, a feat which has never been equalled. By 1920, despite coming second in the US Open when he was aged 50, he had virtually retired to his cottage at South Herts golf club.

Harry Vardon left the world a golf grip named after him, though in truth he did not invent it but popularised it. What he did invent, though, was the upright swing, hitting the ball straighter than any of his contemporaries, particularly with the long and middle irons and woods. Paintings and photographs of him show his long, flowing follow-through to a high finish. Despite his prowess off the tee and fairway, he was reputed to be a miserable putter, suffering the 'yips' on very short putts.

He died on 20 March 1937 and is buried in Totteridge parish church.

James Braid

James Braid was the third member of the 'Great Triumvirate' which virtually ruled golf during the last years of the 19th century and the early part of the 20th, Vardon and JH Taylor being the other two. Between them, these three won the British Open 16 times in 20 years up to the outbreak of World War I.

Braid was the only Scot among the three, born at Earlsferry in Fife on 6 February 1870. He developed a little later than the other two, not winning his first Open until 1901 at Muirfield, despite having played in the event every year since 1896, the year he turned professional. Until then he had worked as a joiner before moving to London as a clubmaker in the Army & Navy Stores. During his time as a joiner he had suffered an accident to his left eye, getting lime in it which was to affect his sight in later years.

Braid had to wait four years for his next victory, at St Andrews in 1905; in 1906 he won again, then again in 1908, shattering the existing Open scoring record with a 291 – 70, 77, 72, 72. Until then winning scores in the 80s had been common. The record stood until 1927, by which time equipment and golf ball technology had moved on some way.

His 1910 victory made him the first man to win the title five times, though that was equalled the following year by Vardon, who went on to win a sixth title. Braid, however, won the British Matchplay Championship – second only in importance to the Open itself – in 1903, 1905,

1907 and 1911, something his contemporaries never did. He even fought his way through to the final of that event as late as 1927, when he was 57 years old.

By this time, though, his eyes were troubling him and although he retired to live at Walton Heath, south of London, he continued to come out on his birthday every year to 'beat his age' – something he normally did.

After the First World War he turned his hand more to designing golf courses than playing them. The brace of courses at Gleneagles – the King's and the Queen's – are among his best, a lasting testament to the genius of the man. Carnoustie, Rosemount and Dalmahoy were also fashioned by him.

He was also instrumental in starting the Professional Golfers' Association, remaining interested in its activities right up to his death on 27 November 1950.

Bobby Jones

Robert Tyre Jones Jnr was born in Atlanta, Georgia on 17 March 1902 – St Patrick's Day. The family was fairly comfortable and young Bobby began playing golf at the East Lake course when he was about five, using a cut-down club and following his parents around as they played, just hitting the odd ball down the fairway.

His ball-striking became highly proficient and by the time he was 14 he had won the Georgia State Open; a year later he won the Southern Amateur Championship.

His break into the big time came in 1921 when, although losing in the fourth round of the British Amateur championship, he played in the match between Britain and the United States which led to the foundation of the Walker Cup. That visit had its downside, though; for, disgusted with his play in the Open at St Andrews, he picked up his ball halfway through a round and stalked off, something he regretted for years after.

Then began a fairytale of success. In 1923 he won the US Open after a play-off; in 1924 and 1925 the US Amateur; in 1926 he collected the British Open and the US Open; 1927 brought the British Open and the US Amateur; 1928 the US

Bobby Jones. In 1930 he won the US and British Amateur championships and the US and British Open championships.

Amateur and 1929 the US Open. In 1930 came the crowning glory – the British Open, the US Open, the British Amateur and the US Amateur, a grand slam that has never been equalled. (Only four players have won the British and US Opens in the same year: Sarazen (1932), Hogan (1953), Trevino (1971) and Watson (1982). They were all professionals.)

By then, Jones had also played in 10 Walker Cup matches, winning all bar one – a foursome. But having scaled this everest, he retired from competitive golf. There was intense speculation as to the reasons, but Jones himself decided that he could do no better than the Grand Slam – he was also emotionally drained and felt unable to take any more. He was 28.

What makes his contribution to golf all the more remarkable is that unlike his contemporaries, he was, and remained, an amateur, though few

professionals relished the prospect of playing him.

He often played with the great Tommy Armour in exhibition matches and gave him two or three strokes a round, 'to make a go of it', as Armour himself later admitted. Jones' philosophy on golf is still worth recounting, for whatever the state of play and however well his opponent might be doing – and we must recall that most matches then were matchplay, not strokeplay – he always had in his mind to beat 'Old Man Par'.

Retirement brought many business opportunities and he became quite a rich man. He maintained his interest in golf, naturally, and it was largely at his instigation that the US Masters was inaugurated in 1934.

Bobby Jones played golf of the highest calibre and his books on golf are still relevant today, 60 years later, for their forthrightness and authority. During his all too few years at the top he beat every major competitor. Sarazen and Hagen, two of the greatest golfers at that time, never beat him between 1922 and 1930.

After 1947 he gave up golf completely, primarily because he fell prey to a wasting, spinal disease which had him confined to a wheelchair, often in great pain. He continued to live in the 'Jones Cabin' at Augusta, a lovely house specially built for him in the grounds of that famous golf club.

In 1958 he was made a Freeman of St Andrews and an Honorary Member of the R and A; the 10th hole on the Old Course is named after him. Bobby Jones died in 1971.

Francis Ouimet

In the early years of this century, golf in America was dominated by the British; either visitors such as Vardon and Taylor or expatriate Scots who had left the old country to seek their fame and fortune across the Atlantic – for several years just after the turn of the century the US Open was won by Willie Anderson, originally from North Berwick, who had emigrated at the age of 15 and made quite a name for himself in the United States.

It was not until 1911 that the US had its first home-grown champion, Jimmy McDermott from Philadelphia taking the title and retaining it the following year. The year after that, however, a young man of just 20 from the Boston suburb of Brookline played through the qualifying rounds and found himself in the tournament proper. In the first round he began poorly – 6, 6, 5, – before getting into gear and finishing in 77. He then had two rounds of 74 to share the lead with the English professionals Harry Vardon and Ted Ray, both of whom, strangely, were born in Jersey.

The final round began badly for the young American, going to the turn in 43, but he then improved and found himself needing to hit one under par on the last four holes. He got his birdie on the 17th to tie with Vardon and Ray.

The American public were fired by this young man but nobody gave him a chance in the 18-hole play-off the next day. By the turn the three were level. But then the young man pulled ahead at the 10th, got an extra one at the 12th, another at the 15th and a final one at the 17th to be four ahead with one to play. Francis Ouimet, an amateur, was the US Open Champion, aged just 20.

Although he won only two more major titles, the US Amateur Championship in 1914 and 1931, and like Bobby Jones never turned professional, he changed America's attitude to golf, proving that the British could be beaten. More than any other player, Francis Ouimet set the imagination of the American golf-watching public alight, perhaps because he was just an ordinary player, not the product of a rich, country-club family background.

Although he had begun his golfing 'career' by caddying, he had to give that up when he was 16 and take a 'real' job – caddies over 16 years of age were considered to be professional golfers then.

After his US Open victory he continued to play amateur golf, playing in every Walker Cup team between 1922 and 1934, and then captaining the team from then until 1949. His finest honour came in 1951 when he was made the first-ever American Captain of the Royal and Ancient Golf Club. He died in 1967.

Right: Walter Hagen was a great golfer whose snappy dressing and business acumen brought him success off the course, too.

Walter Hagen

Rochester, New York in December is a very cold place, and into its snow-filled landscape, just four days before Christmas 1892, Walter Christian Hagen was born.

He came relatively late to tournament golf; his first US Open in 1913 – Ouimet's US Open – was only the second tournament he had ever played in. He was then aged 20. He came fourth that year behind the trio of Ouimet, Vardon and Ray who tied for the play-off.

The following year at Midlothian, Illinois, he did even better, winning with a four-round score of 290. In 1919 he repeated his victory, then decided it was time, the war now being over, to visit Europe – primarily Britain.

Hagen first appeared in the British Open in 1920 at Deal, causing more of a sensation off the course than on it with his 53rd place. What attracted attention to him was the fact that, as professionals were not then allowed in the clubhouse, he hired a Rolls-Royce with chauffeur and used it as a makeshift changing room – parked right outside the clubhouse entrance! He was also the first golfer to take fashion seriously, with his colour-coordinated outfits and black and white brogues.

The following year at St Andrews saw him coming sixth, obviously growing accustomed to links golf. The year after that, 1922 at Sandwich, he won. He only came second the following year before winning the title again in 1924 at Hoylake. In 1926 he was third. Then came two Bobby Jones victories before Hagen took his tally to four in 1928 and 1929, his last British victories.

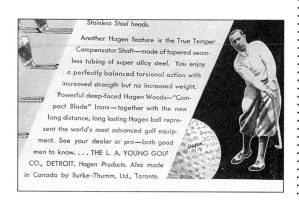

In the meantime he had added the US PGA title in 1921, 1924, 1925, 1926 and 1927, the only man ever to win four consecutive titles in any major other than Tom Morris Jnr in the British Open (1868–72).

A superb player on the course, Hagen was larger than life off it, living a life of some luxury, invariably arriving at tournaments with a limousine and chauffeur, and staying in the plushest hotels. Many a story has been told of his late-night wining and dining; he was always very fashion-conscious, setting trends that were followed by others later. He was, too, a supreme self-publicist, always willing to give an interview to the Press; wherever he went he was attended by great crowds, drawn to him by that certain aura which made him, in his way, the first golfing superstar. He died in October 1969.

Tommy Armour

Tommy Armour, born in Edinburgh in 1895, was the last Scot born and bred in Scotland to win the Open. He was totally besotted by golf and used to travel to see Braid, Vardon and Taylor play exhibition matches all over Scotland. He even had lessons from Vardon, showing how approachable golf 'stars' were in those days.

During the First World War, Armour (!) was called up, finishing as a major in the Tank Corps; however, he suffered injuries and lost the sight of one eye, something which did not stop him perfecting his golf.

In 1920 he won a Scottish Amateur competition at Gleneagles and the French Amateur, and came close to victory in the Canadian Open, losing only in a play-off. He then went to America where Walter Hagen helped him find work in the exclusive Westchester club where he became social secretary at the then enormous salary of $10 000 a year.

By 1924 he had turned professional, winning his first title in 1925 and the US Open and Canadian Open two years after that. In 1930 he won the US PGA title. The following year he returned home to Scotland, but only for a brief visit, during which he won the British Open at Carnoustie, the first time the championship had

been held there. He shot a 71 on the final afternoon.

Returning to his adopted home, the United States, he concentrated more on teaching than playing, moving south to the Florida sunshine and the exotic, pink-stone buildings of Boca Raton where he was professional for many years. Whilst there he gave lessons to the members at $100 an hour, reputedly the highest rate in America. He also wrote a bestselling golf book which is still valid today. Tommy Armour died in 1968.

Ben Hogan – the only man ever to win three Majors in a year.

Ben Hogan

Ben Hogan was born on 13 August 1912 in the Dublin suburb of Fort Worth, Texas. He caddied as a boy, alongside Byron Nelson, but took to golf rather later in life than most other professionals. Indeed, by the time Hogan won his first major title, Nelson had retired!

Hogan had a terrible hook which left him in all sorts of trouble. However, he was determined to rid himself of it and spent months on end practising, emerging with a slice which he then learned to control, giving him a shot which went straight with just a hint of fade at the end. His determination was shown in other ways, too, for in February 1949 his car hit a bus and he was so seriously injured that it was thought he would never walk again. Both his legs were broken, as was his collarbone and pelvis.

Yet not only did he walk, he went on to win the US Open the following year for the second time, having previously won it in 1948. That 1950 win was a victory over pain as well as the golf course, for Hogan had to play his last two rounds in one day, then come back the following morning for an 18-hole play-off. He literally limped round the course but emerged victorious.

His first major title had come in 1946 when he was aged 34 – a time when many professionals had retired from top golf. That was the US PGA, a title he won again in 1948 along with his first US Open.

When he was winning he was winning well, for in 1951 he won both the US Open and the Masters and in 1953 he not only repeated those wins but added the British Open at Carnoustie – the only time he ever entered the British!

That year, 1953, was his high point, despite pain and age beginning to get to him. He played only five tournaments all year and won every one.

Nobody had ever won three majors in one year before – nor have they since. Had the US PGA not still been a matchplay event he would probably have won that too, but he felt that 36 holes a day for four days was just too much for him.

After that year he won no more titles, his putting touch deserting him. Yet the rest of his game still remains an ideal that many young professionals aspire to. More than any other man his ball-striking ability was the nearest to perfect remembered by those fortunate to have seen him play.

Gene Sarazen won the US Open and US PGA in 1922, his first year as a professional, and went on to win all four Majors in the next ten years.

Gene Sarazen

Eugene Saraceni was born in Harrison, New York, to Italian immigrant parents on 27 February 1902. By 1920, when he turned professional, he had anglicised his name to Gene Sarazen. Ironically he had only taken to golf on doctor's orders, having joined his father in the family business straight from school. He was, though, advised to get out of the office into the fresh air and began caddying – a step towards professional golf at the time.

His first professional year brought scant reward; it was in 1922, however, that he made his name. At the start of the last round of the US Open he was barely in contention but came good with a 68, having then to sit it out in the clubhouse as the later starters came in. One by one they faltered, Bobby Jones among them, until there was no-one left. At 20 years old, Gene Sarazen was US Open Champion.

He proved it was no flash in the pan by going on to take the US PGA title a couple of months later, the first time that particular double had been

achieved in the same year. Only Hogan and Nicklaus have equalled that record since.

The year after, he retained the PGA title beating Walter Hagen at the 38th hole of the final. Then came a few years in the wilderness as he tried to rebuild his swing, or rather his grip, for it was not good enough to stand the pressure of golf at the top.

Months of practice paid off in 1932 when he won the British Open at the Prince's course, Sandwich. By this time he had cured his grip problems and had also become a highly proficient sand player – he is credited with having invented the sand wedge the previous winter. He led the Open from the first round, coming home five strokes in front of the field.

He sailed back home to New York for the US Open and won that too, with a closing round of 66, becoming one of only a handful of players to have won both Opens in the same year.

The following year he won the US PGA again but perhaps his most dramatic moment came in the 1935 Masters at Augusta. Craig Wood was already in the clubhouse, seemingly unbeatable with a three-stroke lead over Sarazen who was still out on the course.

Sarazen, playing with Hagen, had driven at the 485-yard 15th. For his second shot he took out a 4-wood and drove it ferociously 250 yards onto the front of the green. It bounced a couple of times, rolled towards the flag at the back of the green, and dropped. An albatross! Sarazen had levelled, and went on to win the play-off, thanks to the shot of a lifetime.

It was the last major victory of his career but until 1991, when aged 89, he was still the honorary starter of the Masters, driving the first ball down the fairway. He was still smiling then, too.

Sam Snead

Sam Snead was born in Hot Springs, Virginia, on 27 May 1912, the same year as Ben Hogan and Byron Nelson – obviously a vintage year.

His boyhood was not eased by an excess of money like some of the golfers who made good, for young Sam actually cut himself a club from a

Sam Snead – the US Open was the only Major to elude him.

branch of swamp maple and shot 72 with it. Much of his early golfing prowess came from his fine athleticism; even into old age he could still pick a ball out of the cup without bending his knees.

He turned professional in 1934 but took a long time to win his first major championship. A few tournament titles came along the way, all adding up to give him a career total of 84 US event wins, seven of them majors.

That first major came in 1942 on the Seaview course overlooking the bay at Atlantic

City, New Jersey, now the eastern seaboard's version of Las Vegas. It was that year that the US PGA came to Seaview and Snead won it, beating Jim Turnesa 2 and 1 in the final. It was the first of three US PGA titles for him, the others coming in 1949 and 1951.

Sam also won the British Open, just once, at St Andrews in 1946, its first year back after the war, scoring 290; which, strangely, was the same score that had won for R Burton in the final pre-war year, 1939.

His other three majors came in the Masters at Augusta, in 1949, 1952 and 1954. He was, though, never to win the US Open, a title he came so close to capturing on many occasions. Yet it remained elusive and he could not complete his own 'grand slam' and win all four majors.

Sam's longevity in golf was, and is, a legend. Even when he was in his sixties he could still get round in under 70 – at 70 he went round a course in 60!

Henry Cotton

Henry Cotton was born in 1907 into a well-off family, his father owning an iron foundry. Henry went to a public school in fashionable Dulwich, South London, but found the golf course preferable to the classroom and left at 17 instead of going on to university, like so many of his fellows.

His father had earlier taken him to be seen by JH Taylor – the great man had muttered something about 'great promise', which was enough encouragement to persuade Henry to become an assistant professional at Fulwell, near Twickenham; but by the time he was 19 he had been appointed professional at Langley Park, Kent, where he had time and space to practise.

That year, 1926, also saw him enter his first Open, at Royal Lytham, the year Bobby Jones won his first title. Jones won it again the following year at St Andrews, Cotton coming a creditable eighth.

A couple of years later he had gone off to become the professional at the Royal Waterloo golf club just outside Brussels, where continental attitudes to professional golfers were more tolerant and in his case almost adulatory, a far cry from their status in Britain.

It was not until 1934, though, that Henry Cotton really made his name in golf with a sensational first two rounds at the Open, held that year at Sandwich. His 67–65 remains a record. The 65 was so good that a golf ball, the Dunlop 65, was named after it. Inevitably Cotton won that Open, adding a further two titles in 1937 and 1948.

Sir Henry Cotton, three times British Open champion, who died just nine days before his knighthood was awarded.

During the war he served as an RAF officer, taking him away from golf for almost six years and possibly robbing him of further major victories. After the 1948 Open at Muirfield, watched by King George VI – the only time a reigning monarch has been to the Open – Cotton gave up tournament golf and concentrated on teaching, writing about golf, building courses and living a life of some style.

He was also one of the founders of the Golf Foundation, established in Britain to encourage youngsters to take up golf. He further instituted the Henry Cotton Rookie of the Year Award in 1960 for the most promising young professional,

THE GREATS: PAST & PRESENT

an award subsequently won by Sandy Lyle and Tony Jacklin among others.

He was elected an honorary member of the R and A in 1968, one of an elite few in the professional game thus honoured. A greater honour was to come though, when his country, in the New Year's Honours List published on 1 January 1988, knighted him – Sir Henry Cotton. Tragically, just nine days before, he had passed away. Aware that the honour was forthcoming, he did not live long enough to enjoy it. The knighthood was granted posthumously.

Peter Thomson

This century only one man has ever won the British Open three times running: Peter Thomson. Thomson was born on 23 August 1929 in Melbourne, Australia, and spent his golfing apprenticeship in the southern hemisphere, winning several not unimportant events before finally coming to Europe to contest the 1951 British Open at Portrush, the only time the event was ever held in Ireland. On that occasion he came sixth, the lowest he was to come for many years.

The following year at Lytham he was second, and again the year after that. In 1954 the Open came to Royal Birkdale for the first time and Thomson relished the tight fairways which suited his game so well, for although he was not a long hitter, he was deadly accurate, often using a 3-wood off the tee to keep the ball in play. This accuracy, often sacrificing distance, was the main reason he failed to make much of an impact in the United States where wide, watered fairways put such a premium on distance.

At Birkdale he stayed with the early leaders and came to the last round believing he needed a 70 to win. He reached the turn in 35 and needed

a four at the last to get his 70. His iron to the green found a bunker and he just missed the putt, but showed his relaxed attitude to golf by casually knocking the ball in back-handed for a final total of 283. Nobody caught him.

The following year at St Andrews he bettered that by two, then won again at Hoylake in 1956 to become the first man this century to gain three Opens in a row. Tension at St Andrews in 1957 was high, with Thomson poised to equal the record of four in a row set by Young Tom Morris over a century earlier.

It was not to be. Thomson lost out on the Open, and that record, by three shots, though not without a minor controversy on the final green. Bobby Locke, Thomson's contemporary and great rival, was three ahead when he came to putt on the 72nd green. Because his ball was on a fellow competitor's line he placed his marker a putter-head's length away. Replacing it and knowing a fourth Open victory was his, he forgot to move the marker back to its correct position. The incident was reported by onlookers but the Committee decreed that the result should stand, the margin being more than the one-stroke penalty that should have been incurred.

Thomson was not finished yet, however, for the following year, back at Hoylake, he equalled Locke's four victories, going on in 1965 at Birkdale, the scene of his first victory, to gain his fifth, one of only five men ever to achieve that feat.

By the early sixties Thomson's lack of distance off the tee had been largely superseded by the long hitting of Arnold Palmer and the up and coming Jack Nicklaus. Thomson, although only in his thirties, retired with grace, though he was tempted onto the US Seniors tour in the early 1980s, winning prodigiously over a couple of years before returning to Melbourne to spend more time writing and designing golf courses.

Modern Greats

Arnold Palmer

British Open: 1961, 1962
US Open: 1960
Masters: 1958, 1960, 1962, 1964

Arnold Palmer brought a new dimension to golf in the 1960s at the same time that television was beaming the sport to audiences throughout America and the world. The combination became irresistible.

Palmer's game was based on raw power and he had the build for it – large hands, enormous forearms and broad shoulders. His quick swing with its abbreviated follow through made the purists shudder. But it got results, even when his big-hitting finished in deep trouble. He had the strength to blast the ball out of deep rough, and the finesse to conjure the ball out of the trees, over a lake and float it down beside the pin. In addition, he was a bold putter, rapping the ball into the hole from all parts of the green or leaving it four feet past and rattling in the return.

Arnold Palmer. His exciting golf hooked millions of television viewers to the game.

Multi-million dollar golfers – Jack Nicklaus (left), Palmer and Greg Norman at the 1990 Masters.

Wherever he went Palmer was followed by admiring galleries – Arnie's Army became part of golfing legend.

His golfing philosophy was simple: 'If I can see the ball I can hit it. If I can hit it I can hole it.' He scowled and grimaced a lot as he surveyed a difficult shot, then with a final hitch of the trousers he would take the club from the bag and hit the shot without wasting any time. A face-splitting grin was never hidden far beneath the surface and his gracious, self-effacing manner in victory or defeat made him an ideal ambassador for a new and exciting era in the game.

At a time when the Open Championship in Britain was at its lowest ebb, having become a domestic and Commonwealth affair, Palmer's victories in the early 1960s and his insistence on playing every year convinced many leading American professionals that they too should try to win the oldest championship in the world.

Palmer won all his majors in a short period and could never do better than second in the US PGA, denying him the elusive grand slam of the four major championships. But he has continued to play his own brand of attacking golf for more than 30 years and has once again worked his magic in helping to build the American seniors tour into a massive spectacle which rivals the main tour for public support.

Gary Player

British Open: 1959, 1968, 1974
US Open: 1965
Masters: 1961, 1974, 1978
US PGA: 1962, 1972

Gary Player spent months practising shot after shot.

When he first arrived in Britain at the age of 19, Gary Player was armed with a hooker's grip, a flat swing, a burning desire to learn from the leading players and a fierce determination to succeed. One prominent British player advised him to go back to South Africa and find some other means of making a living.

This only encouraged him to spend more and more hours on the practice ground. Acting on advice from Dai Rees he weakened his grip and the following year he won the Dunlop Masters at Sunningdale with a score of 270 which included two rounds of 64.

He worked hard to build up his physique to make up for his short stature and developed a practice and fitness routine which he still maintains. Every practice session would have a target – no lunch until 20 seven-iron shots finished within a nine-foot circle, no dinner until he had holed a bunker shot. Each time a target was achieved he made the next day's target a little more difficult.

In this way he made himself one of the world's finest golfers where many had given him no hope. His short game in particular was superb and he was rightly rated the game's finest bunker player.

At the end of a tournament in which he had holed out from a bunker he was asked about his 'lucky' shot. 'It's a funny thing,' replied Player, 'but the more I practise, the luckier I get.'

He became a truly international golfer, winning his own South African Open 13 times, the Australian championship on seven occasions, plus a string of titles in Britain, Europe and America. He once recorded a round of 59 in the Brazilian Open.

His determination was a major factor in winning the 1959 Open at Muirfield. With two rounds to be played on the last day, he was eight shots behind the leader, but finished with rounds of 70 and 68 for a two-shot victory. He went on

Right: *'The more I practise the luckier I get.' Player, still practising and still lucky, won the British Senior Open in 1990.*

to win all four of the major championships which constitute the modern grand slam.

He has now carried his fiercely competitive golf game into the senior ranks where, after winning the Senior Open, he went back to the practice ground and then out on to the course in the gathering darkness to ensure that he had correctly cured a bad shot which had almost cost him the title.

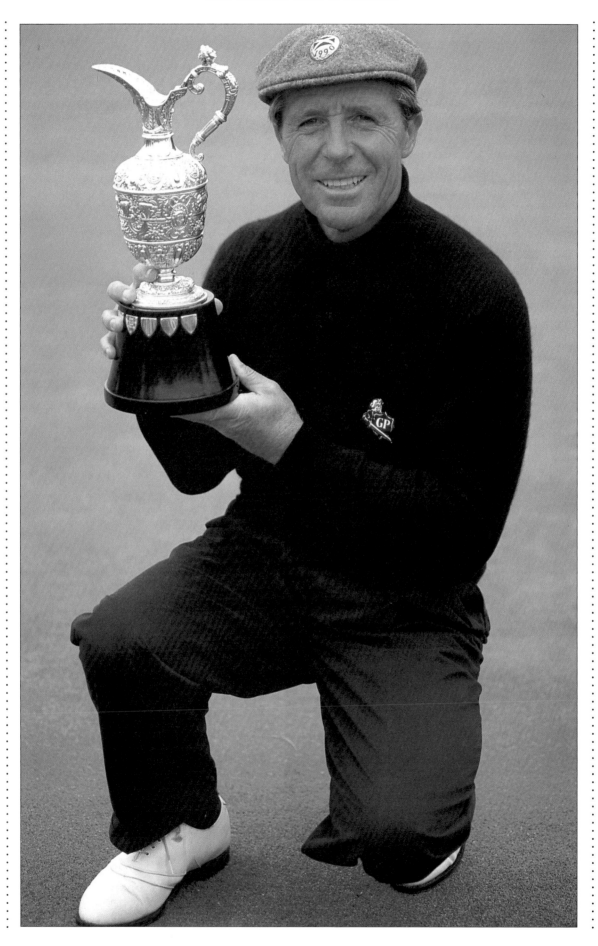

Jack Nicklaus

British Open: 1966, 1970, 1978
US Open: 1962, 1967, 1972, 1980
Masters: 1963, 1965, 1966, 1972, 1975, 1986
US PGA: 1963, 1971, 1973, 1975, 1980

If the winning of the four major events is the true yardstick of a champion's ability then Jack Nicklaus holds a position which is unlikely ever to be challenged. His total of 18 victories puts him head and shoulders above any credible opposition. Walter Hagen collected 11 titles in the 1920s, Ben Hogan and Gary Player won nine each. Tom Watson has eight.

In addition to the professional titles Nicklaus has two US Amateur Championships to his credit, the first of which he won at the age of 19 in 1959. The following year he set a new amateur record

Eighteen Major titles put Jack Nicklaus firmly at the top of the list of golf's greatest.

in the American Open, finishing second to Arnold Palmer with rounds of 71–71–69–71.

It was to be another year before he joined the professional ranks, but he immediately incurred the wrath of the American golfing public by winning the US Open. The idea of this pudgy, crew-cut youngster beating the people's hero in a play-off was unthinkable. It was not until years later, when he had lost weight and grown his hair and Palmer had left the stage, that Nicklaus was fully accepted in his own country.

In his second season he won the Masters and the PGA and just missed getting into a play-off for the Open at Lytham. His hoard of major titles was building fast. Probably the victory which gave him most satisfaction was the Open Championship at St Andrews in 1970. He had set his heart on winning the Open at the home of golf and the chance nearly slipped from his grasp. The

Left: *'The Bear' lines up a putt at the 1986 World Matchplay championships.*

unfortunate Doug Sanders missed a three-foot putt for a win on the final green and Nicklaus clinched the title in an 18-hole play-off the next day.

But perhaps the most impressive aspect of his string of major titles is the length of the period in which they have been won. His first and last victories are separated by 25 years – and in the 100 majors that Nicklaus has played in that time, he has finished in the top three 45 times.

When he passed his 50th birthday he celebrated by winning his first tournament on the senior tour, but then went straight to Augusta and finished sixth in the Masters. It is not beyond the bounds of possibility that Nicklaus will add further to his outstanding record.

Lee Trevino

British Open: 1971, 1972
US Open: 1968, 1971
US PGA: 1975, 1984

While his contemporaries on the professional tour were making their way into the game through college golf teams and the country club circuit, Lee Trevino was working as a greenkeeper and taking extra jobs as a caddy on his days off to earn money for his family.

The son of an immigrant Mexican grave digger, he had first become aware of golf when the family moved to a four-room shack within sight of the Glen Lakes course in Dallas. He would watch the local golfers and copy their actions in the hay field outside his home. During his time as a greenkeeper he would play a few holes out of sight of the clubhouse as darkness fell, but he did not take up the game until he went into the Marines at the age of 17.

Having played throughout his tour of duty in the Far East, he was able to get a job at the local driving range when he returned home and he supplemented his income by playing money matches, often using only a three-iron to increase the bet.

It was during this period that he developed his uncanny ability to fashion and shape shots in

Fast-talking long-hitting ever-winning Tex-Mex: Lee Trevino.

Trevino (left) – still talking – with Ray Floyd at the British Open.

a way that the professionals of earlier eras had done with their limited range of equipment.

He turned professional in 1960, playing local tournaments and occasionally winning himself a spot on the regular tour. Having qualified for the US Open of 1967 he finished in fifth place and went full-time on the tour the following year.

Virtually unknown to the great American golfing public, he became the first man to break 70 in every round of the Open that year at Oak Hill and snatched the title by four clear shots from Jack Nicklaus. With his sharp mind and quick wit, Trevino became an instant folk hero. He was less popular with many of his fellow pros, who found his constant chatter a distinct disadvantage during competitive rounds.

But there was no denying his playing ability, and in addition to his six major victories he was five times awarded the Vardon Trophy for the lowest scoring average on the American tour. He is now the number one contender on the senior circuit, winning more money in 1990 than the leading player on the regular tour.

Tom Watson

British Open: 1975, 1977, 1980, 1982, 1983
US Open: 1982
Masters: 1977, 1981

When Tom Watson hit his second shot through the green at the 17th hole at St Andrews in the final round of the 1984 Open Championship, his ball finished close to the wall, beyond the road which forms a major hazard at this infamous hole. It signalled the end of a dream.

Watson was tied with Seve Ballesteros with two holes to play and victory would have given him a unique record of three Open titles in consecutive years *and* a total of six, matching the record set by Harry Vardon in 1914.

But it was not to be. He failed to make his par, and when Ballesteros birdied the final hole he took the championship by two shots. Yet in a 10-year period Watson had won the Open five times, a truly dominant performance.

When Watson joined the pro tour after graduating in psychology from Stanford University, he became known as Huckleberry Finn – he had the fresh, open-faced look of the American farm boy. He had a few near misses in his early career,

Tom Watson (left) and Seve Ballesteros, two of the world's best during the 1980s with nine Majors between them.

leading the US Open in 1974 going into the last round but fading badly to finish fifth, and his critics began to doubt that he could jump the final hurdle to victory.

He had always been an admirer of links golf since his first visit to Britain, and it was on one of the toughest courses of them all that he took his first major title, winning the Open Championship of 1975 at Carnoustie. He tied with Australian Jack Newton after four rounds and won the 18-hole play-off by hitting a superb two-iron to the heart of the final green.

But perhaps the highlight of his 10-year run was the final round of the 1977 championship at Turnberry. Tied with Jack Nicklaus at the start of the last day, they were 10 shots ahead of the rest of the field. Nicklaus shot a 66 – and lost by a stroke. In 18 holes of the most exquisite cut-and-thrust golf, Watson went ahead for the first time on the 17th when Nicklaus missed a short putt to match his birdie four. A perfect drive at the last hole, seven-iron to three feet and another birdie gave Watson the title after Nicklaus had holed a monster for a closing three.

Left: *Excellence on the green has helped Watson to five British Open victories.*

Tom has a habit of being in contention at every tournament. Here he is approaching another birdie at the 1989 US PGA.

Nick Faldo

British Open: 1987, 1990
Masters: 1989, 1990

It was the sight of Jack Nicklaus at the Masters, on his parents' new colour television, that inspired sports-mad Nick Faldo to take an interest in the game at the age of 13. A series of six lessons with local pro Ian Connelly fired his enthusiasm and within four years he had been selected for the England youth team. He became the youngest winner of the Amateur Championship at 18.

In his second year as a professional he finished eighth in the order of merit and won a Ryder Cup place. It was to be a dream debut at Lytham in 1977. Faldo teamed up with Peter Oosterhuis for victories over Ray Floyd and Lou Graham in the foursomes and over Floyd and Jack Nicklaus in the fourball series. He rounded off a

The 1991 Ryder Cup proved to be one of the low points in Faldo's otherwise glowing career.

perfect week by beating reigning Masters and Open champion Tom Watson by one hole in the singles. Faldo had played three matches and won three points out of a team total of seven.

By 1983 he had risen to the number one spot in Europe and he became one of the few overseas golfers to win a tour event in America the following year. But he was not satisfied. Despite his undoubted talent, he had not won any of the four major championships and he set out on a two-year plan to rebuild his swing with British golf coach David Leadbetter, who was based in Florida.

The low point came in the 1985 season when Faldo dropped to 42nd place in Europe, but now he climbed steadily back towards towards the top, starting the following season.

A win in the Spanish Open then got him off to a fine start in 1987 and when the Open was played in July, at a very wet and windy Muirfield, he put together rounds of 68–69–71–71 for his breakthrough into the really big time. In the terrible conditions of the final day he scored 18 pars, described by one American commentator as boring but in reality a masterful display of controlled golf.

He went on to score back-to-back victories in the Masters at Augusta and emphasised his position by a five-stroke victory in the 1990 Open at St Andrews with one of the great displays of precision play.

Nick Faldo on his way to his first Masters title, Augusta 1989. He retained the coveted green jacket the following year.

In the final round of the 1990 Masters, Faldo plays out of a greenside bunker on the 12th for another par.

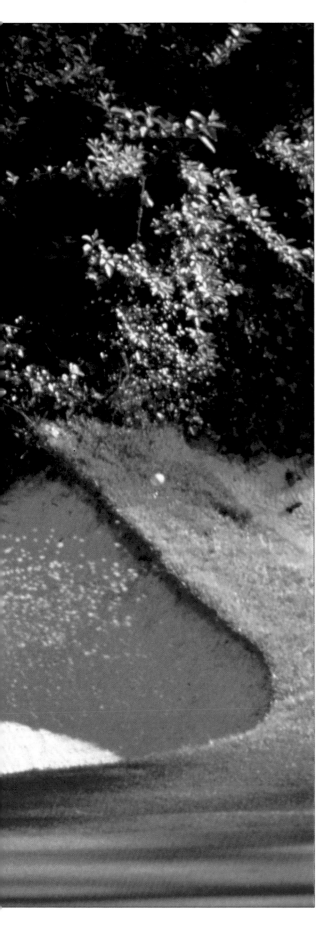

Greg Norman

British Open: 1986

Although he topped the world rankings for longer than any other player and has accumulated an impressive list of worldwide victories, Greg Norman has not come close to realising his potential.

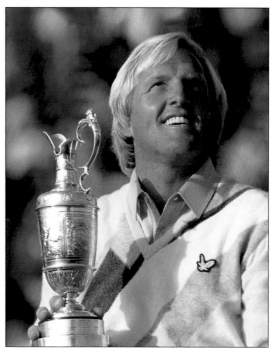

Greg Norman, British Open champion at Turnberry in 1986. The other championships continue to elude the big-hitting Australian.

He started playing golf at the age of 17, got down to scratch in two years, won the fourth tournament he played as a professional and at the end of his first season was picked to represent Australia in the World Cup. He won a tournament in his first year on the European tour and successfully dominated both the European and his home scene for a couple of seasons before heading for America.

Just 10 years after taking up the game for a living, he led the American money-winners in the bitter-sweet season of 1986. He came to the final hole of the Masters needing a par four to tie Jack Nicklaus, but blocked his second shot way into the crowd. He held the lead going into the final round of the US Open, but skidded out of contention with a 75.

Norman on the 17th tee at Turnberry on his way to a course record of 63. Ray Floyd looks on.

accurate with his long clubs. During the course of his career he has become the complete golfer by working extremely hard to bring his short game and putting up to the same standard as his driving. It remains a mystery why such an accomplished golfer has only one championship title to his name.

Severiano Ballesteros

British Open: 1979, 1984, 1988
Masters: 1980, 1983

When the final account of the career of Severiano Ballesteros is written, it will not only recall his many triumphs in major championships or his exciting, attacking brand of golf. It will single him out as the man who inspired an explosion within European golf and who led the charge which broke American domination of the game.

As a youngster, Ballesteros and his three older brothers – who were all destined to become

When he arrived at Turnberry for the British Open he found narrow fairways flanked by waist-deep rough and strong winds whipping across the course. He finally showed that he had all the talent and resilience to capture the biggest prizes with a stunning display of power golf, including a second round 63, which put him five shots ahead of the field.

A month later he was seemingly denied victory in the US PGA when Bob Tway holed a bunker shot at the final hole. But in truth, Norman, having held a big lead with just nine holes to play, had thrown away his chance of the title. The following spring he was robbed of the Masters when Larry Mize holed from 20 yards off the green in their play-off.

Then in the 1989 Open at Troon he was again beaten in a play-off for the title, having come storming up through the field with a final round of 64.

Norman has always had the ability to hit the ball vast distances and he has been remarkably

professionals – caddied at the Santander Club in northern Spain. Just before darkness fell they would creep out of the bushes and play a couple of holes on the deserted course.

Seve played every shot with the only club he had – an ageing three-iron. From the age of eight he learned to play every shot in the game with that club, one minute hooding the face to drive against the wind, the next moment laying the face wide open to float the ball over a bunker.

He developed a genius for shot-making which gave him control of the ball in the manner of Lee Trevino. And he combined that with a ferociously attacking power-game reminiscent of Arnold Palmer.

His audacious talent shone through the British Open Championship at Birkdale in 1976 when he opened with two rounds of 69. His lack of experience prevented him from holding that leading position to the end, but he tied with Jack Nicklaus in second place behind the mercurial Johnny Miller.

But in that year, his third as a professional,

he won two tournaments and headed the European order of merit, still only 19 years old. He was to retain the number one position for three years and was never out of the top 10 for 14 years.

His first Open victory, at Lytham in 1979, was a clear three-shot margin over Nicklaus and Ben Crenshaw. But carping American critics called him the 'car park champion' because of a few off-line tee shots – they had obviously never watched Arnold Palmer play – and were still resentful when he became the youngest ever winner of the US Masters the following spring by a convincing four-shot margin.

Above: *Seve beats Curtis Strange at the 17th during the 1987 Ryder Cup to retain the trophy for Europe.*

Left: *Anguish for Seve at the 10th during the 1988 Masters. Brother Vicente is caddying.*

All smiles for Seve this time after his 9 and 8 victory over Chip Beck in the 1989 World Matchplay.

When Britain's Ryder Cup team was strengthened by bringing European players into the side for the first time in 1979, Ballesteros made an immediate impact and has been a leading force in reversing a long succession of American victories.

Ian Woosnam

Masters: 1991

Although he turned professional in 1976, Ian Woosnam had to make three visits to the qualifying school before he earned his place on the European tour. He then faced a desperate struggle to stay on the tour, earning less than a total of £7000 in four years.

His determination and endless hours of practice paid off in 1982 when he jumped to eighth place in the rankings with close to £50000 in winnings. Over the next four years he climbed steadily into fourth place before exploding onto the world scene in 1987.

He got off to an early season start by taking the Hong Kong Open title, won five times in Europe, including the World Matchplay Championship, and was a member of the Ryder Cup team that recorded the first European victory in America.

He went on to partner David Llewellyn to the first Welsh success in the World Cup and picked up the individual title on the way. In one season, he had won more than £1 million.

That was a hard act to follow, but after a couple of 'disappointing' seasons where his earnings dropped to little more than a quarter of a million pounds, he captured five events in 1990, including the Matchplay title again, and once more was the top player in Europe. But he had still not won the major championship that he craved.

When he stood on the 18th tee in the final round of the Masters at Augusta in 1991, that first major title was almost in his grasp. He needed to make four to win. He hit an enormous drive over the bunker on the left and over the crowd as well. His eight-iron approach found the edge of the

Above: *Ian Woosnam shows poise and class as he splashes from a greenside bunker during the 1987 Cannes Open. The professionals make these bunker shots look deceptively easy.*

Left: *Woosnam gets some advice from his caddy Phil Morbey during the 1991 Ryder Cup at Kiawah Island.*

green, short of the hole, and his first putt slid six feet past. To his eternal credit Woosnam holed the putt across the right-to-left break and finally joined the elite ranks of championship winners. He was also elevated to the top of the world rankings.

The little Welshman who used to travel the circuit in a motor caravan to save on hotel bills now arrives in style in his own aeroplane.

Payne Stewart

US Open: 1991
US PGA: 1989

From the time he joined the US pro circuit in 1979, Payne Stewart seemed destined for greatness. Yet although he was a consistent performer who regularly got into winning positions, it took a full 10 years before he began to realise his potential.

In that decade he had amassed prize-money of more than three million dollars. On average he finished in the top 10 in one tournament out of three. He had won four times on the American circuit and three times in Asia and Australia. But he had also finished second 10 times and lost three play-offs.

Above: *Payne Stewart holds the follow-through in this difficult pitch out of deep rough.*

Left: *A delighted Stewart proudly displays the US PGA trophy, Kemper Lakes 1989 – his first Major.*

In the harsh world of professional golf he was regarded as a man who 'choked' when the pressure was really on – a man who got into winning positions but lacked the final killer instinct. But all the labels that had been tied to him over the years were thrown out of the window when he charged from six shots behind the leader to capture the 1989 US PGA title with a final round of 67. Finally Stewart had started to earn respect as well as money.

He had come close to victory in the British Open at Sandwich in 1985 when again he came up through the field on the final day. His closing 68 set an early target that no one else could match – until Sandy Lyle safely two-putted the last for a one-shot home victory.

He again finished second in the Open, this time to Nick Faldo, at St Andrews in 1990, with three rounds of 68 and a closing 71. But he was not to be denied in his own national championship, played in 1991 at Hazeltine, the scene of Tony Jacklin's US Open triumph 21 years before. Stewart mastered the demanding course and finished tied with Scott Simpson. In the only 18-hole play-off left in the four major championships, he came from two shots behind with three holes to play for a last-ditch victory.

Curtis Strange

US Open: 1988, 1989

The son of a golf professional from Norfolk, Virginia, Curtis Strange has been swinging a golf club since the time he learned to walk. He crowned a successful amateur career with three victories and one halved match in the Walker Cup of 1975 and turned professional the following year.

But the transition was not as smooth as he might have expected. Although he qualified for the tour a year later, he made no impression in his first two seasons. He spent months revising the swing which had been with him since childhood, losing some of his prodigious length but making the action more compact and reliable.

He had come to recognise that keeping the ball in play and hitting a lot of greens in regulation was a more reliable way to get results, and his

Curtis Strange became only the sixth man to win the US Open back to back in 1989 at Oak Hill, New York.

whole attitude to the game became one of striving for consistency rather than relying on an occasional flurry of birdies.

For this reason he became known to his fellow pros as 'The Grinder', regularly grinding out good scores week after week. His winning streak started in 1979 and by the following season he had jumped to third place in the money list. In 1985, 1987 and 1988 he topped that list as he became one of the tour's regular winners.

But the big ones always eluded him. His greatest chance came in the 1985 Masters, where he found the water twice in the closing six holes to finish second.

When he was next in position to win he made the most of his chance. Yet, typically for The Grinder, it was not to be easy. After four rounds of the 1988 US Open at Brookline he was tied with Nick Faldo, but won the 18-hole play-off by a comfortable four-stroke margin.

The following year he came to the top of the field as one contender after another threw away their chances and he became the first winner of consecutive Opens since Ben Hogan 38 years before.

Curtis takes a moment to line up a putt.

Sandy Lyle

British Open: 1985
Masters: 1988

Although he was born in England there was never any doubt in Sandy Lyle's mind that he was as Scottish as his parents and that he would play for Scotland as a professional golfer.

Alex Lyle was professional at Hawkstone Park and young Sandy grew up with a natural ability for the game. He was Amateur Strokeplay champion at the age of 17, but his final act as an amateur, in the Walker Cup of 1977, was hugely disappointing. He played three times and lost all his matches.

But he immediately won the tour qualifying school and then took the Nigerian Open title, which included a round of 61. In his second year among the professionals he led the order of merit, and for a seven-year period he was three times the leading player in Europe and never fell below fifth place.

In 1980 he won the individual title in the World Cup and he had scored victories in Japan

and Hawaii by the time he arrived at Royal St George's for the 1985 Open Championship. Rounds of 68, 71 and 73 left him three shots behind the leaders on the last day, but he moved up through the field with a fine run of holes on the homeward stretch and although he took three to get down from the edge of the last green, he had done enough to become the first home winner for 16 years.

Above: *Sandy Lyle on the tee at the 1988 Suntory World Matchplay.*

Left: *Happier days! Lyle the Open champion at Royal St George's in 1985, the first British winner since Tony Jacklin.*

Four wins in America, including the Tournament Players' Championship, preceded his appearance in the 1988 Masters at Augusta. The lead he had established after three rounds had evaporated by the time he reached the 13th tee, thanks to three putts at the 11th and a shot into the water at the short 12th.

By the final hole he needed a birdie three to win the title, but drove into the massive bunker on the left of the fairway. He then unleashed the shot of the year – a stunning seven-iron from the sand which carried over the flag, bit into the green and came back down the slope to 12 feet. He rolled in the putt to become the first British player to capture the Masters.

By the time he went back to defend his title, his individualistic swing had gone off the boil and he failed to qualify for the final two rounds. He suffered two seasons of purgatory before his game gave signs of coming back to life in 1991.

Bernhard Langer

Masters: 1985

Coming from a country with a limited number of courses and no history of producing tournament professionals, Bernhard Langer has transformed the game in Germany and added considerably to the explosion of golf in Europe.

Although he turned professional in 1972, his early efforts on the tour came to nothing, but his undoubted talent was on show when he won the Under-25 Championship in 1979 by no less than 17 strokes. The following year he won the Dunlop Masters and finished the season with £32000 for ninth place in the rankings.

He moved from there to the number one spot in 1981, the year he won the first of his three German Open titles. He played his way into the

Ryder Cup team that season and has held his place since, becoming one of the key figures in defeating the Americans at home and away. In the close matches at PGA National in Florida in 1983, when Europe lost by just one point, Langer played in five matches and collected four points.

After heading the European money list again in 1984, Langer decided to spend more time on the American circuit the following season. He had a few reasonable results in the early events and then dented American morale by becoming the second European to win the Masters, following Seve Ballesteros' triumphs in 1980 and 1983.

Langer's fine record in more than 10 years of top level golf has come despite recurring putting problems. He suffers at regular intervals with the 'yips' – an involuntary stab at the ball, particularly on short putts. He has overcome the problem with a variety of cures which have included placing the left hand below the right and his latest, where the right hand clamps the top of the putter grip to the left wrist.

Most good players who have had the 'yips' never recover. Langer has come back three times and in the process made himself such a superb performer on the greens that in 1990 he was the leading putter in Europe, averaging only 28.69 putts per round.

Langer appears to have conquered the yips again with this unorthodox putting grip.

Bernhard Langer – a colourful player on and off the course.

Langer takes the picturesque route to the green at Wentworth during the 1989 Volvo PGA.

Above: *Paul Broadhurst opened his Ryder Cup career in 1991 by winning both his matches. Here he takes advice from team-mate Ian Woosnam.*

Right: *The confident swing of a promising young golfer.*

STARS OF THE FUTURE

Paul Broadhurst

To finance his days in amateur golf, Paul Broadhurst took on jobs in a factory, as a gardener and driving a van. At the end of 1988, after winning the Lytham Trophy, winning a place in the England team and collecting the gold medal as leading amateur in the Open Championship, he turned professional and won his tour card at the first attempt.

He finished third in the Desert Classic and the Jersey Open before winning his first tour title in his rookie year with rounds of 65, 70 and 72 in the rain-shortened Cannes Open. His first season was cut short when he had to undergo surgery to his left hand.

It took some time for him to pick up the threads in 1990, but he finished the season well with another victory and more than £100 000 in official winnings.

Although he won the European Pro-Celebrity event in early August of 1991, Broadhurst was still well short of the place he coveted in the Ryder Cup team, which was to be finalised two weeks later at the German Open. In that event Broadhurst closed with a round of 65, which included two eagle threes and birdies at the final two holes to tie Mark McNulty. He lost the play-off at the first extra hole, but jumped into ninth spot in the order of merit and gained automatic entry into the Ryder Cup.

Team captain Bernard Gallacher kept Broadhurst in reserve until the second day fourball matches when he was paired with Ian Woosnam for a vital victory. And he showed what an asset he was to the team on the final day with a convincing 3 and 1 win over Mark O'Meara. Played two and won two is a great record to carry forward to the next encounter.

John Daly

On the day before the start of the 1991 US PGA Championship, over the monstrous course at Crooked Stick, Indiana, John Daly, a rookie professional who had enjoyed a moderately good year in the pro ranks, was getting twitchy. At the start of the week he had been eighth reserve for the event and hadn't given much thought to that many players dropping out, but six had already fallen by the wayside.

When a telephone call told him that number seven had gone the same way and that Nick Price would definitely not play if the birth of his child was imminent, Daly took the bull by the horns, packed his car and set off through the night.

Above: *Instant reactions for television from John Daly as he reflects on his amazing success in the 1991 US PGA.*

Left: *Long John had out-hit every player at Crooked Stick in a truly stunning display of golf.*

The drive from Memphis in Tennessee took until 1.30 in the morning. He grabbed a few hours' sleep and reported at the club to discover that he was in the field.

With absolutely no preparation and no chance to assess the course he went straight into his big-hitting routine and came back with a first round 69. While all the other pros were complaining about the 7289-yard monster course, Daly just kept smashing it into submission. In the events he had played on the US tour earlier in the year his average driving distance was 286 yards. At Crooked Stick he opened up a little and averaged over 303 yards off every tee.

With that sort of power he was hitting way beyond the problems that faced most of the other competitors. He achieves his distance with an extraordinary backswing, getting the hands extremely high and keeping the left arm very straight, with the clubhead dropping below the level of his left knee. He generates enormous clubhead speed and during the week of the championship he refused to let the pressure make him cut down on his power.

With rounds of 69, 67, 69 and 71 he kept his composure for a three-stroke winning margin, one of the few players to open his tournament account with a major victory.

Robert Gamez

So eager was he to represent his country in the Walker Cup matches of 1989 that Robert Gamez delayed his decision to turn pro, even though he was not assured of a place in the team. It was a bitter-sweet departure from the amateur ranks, Gamez coming from behind in his final singles match and chipping in for a winning birdie on the final hole against Stephen Dodd, only for the Americans to be beaten on home soil for the first time.

If he left the amateurs on a low note, Gamez joined the professional ranks in a blaze of glory. In the Tucson Open in Arizona in January of 1990 his first professional round was a 65. He followed with a 66 and then a 69 and although he slumped to a 70 on the final day, driving into a bunker and three-putting the final hole, he was still four shots clear of the field, which was led by the then British Open champion Mark Calcavecchia.

Within three months Gamez was at it again, this time in the prestigious Nestle Invitational at Arnold Palmer's Bay Hill course in Florida. If the Tucson event had not attracted a full house of the world's leading players, they were certainly out in force this time – all the top Americans, plus Greg

Norman, Nick Faldo, Ian Woosnam and José Maria Olazabal.

This time Gamez reversed his scoring pattern, starting with a 71 and coming down through 69 and 68 to a final round of 66 to beat Norman into second place by one shot. It was not just the fact of this win, but its manner, which caught the imagination.

At the final hole, needing a birdie to give him the chance of a play-off with Norman, he holed a full seven-iron second shot to snatch an unbelievable victory.

At the end of his first year as a professional, Gamez had climbed to 27th place in the American money list with almost half a million dollars – a stunning rookie performance.

Below: *Robert Gamez at the Million Dollar Challenge, Sun City. He made half a million dollars in his first season.*

Above: *Gamez, undoubtedly one of America's brightest rising stars.*

'How did that miss?' Gamez typically takes it in his stride.

Phil Mickleson

If his father is to be believed, Phil Mickleson was swinging a golf club left-handed at the age of two while he was still in nappies. Certainly by the time he was 10 he had collected his first major title – the World Junior Championship. Over a par-three course, Mickleson's six-under-par total left the opposition trailing.

Many other titles were to fall to the tall left-hander with the slightly over-long, flowing swing, the most important being the United States Amateur Championship in 1990. He led the qualifiers with a two-round total of 135, and in the final he played some stunning golf to defeat his former Arizona State University team-mate Manny Zerman by 5 and 4. Mickleson birdied five of the last 12 holes and was five under par for the 32 holes of the final.

Although he has no intention of turning professional before finishing his psychology degree, Mickleson took the chance of an outing with the pros during the 1991 Tucson Open. After opening rounds of 65, 71 and 65 he led on the final day until

Left-hander Phil Mickleson won his first title when he was only ten years old.

Still an amateur, Mickleson is one of the most exciting prospects to come out of the United States.

the desert scrub grabbed him at the par-five 14th. He took penalty drops twice on the way to an eight, but then birdied the 16th and rattled in a nine-foot birdie putt on the last to win by a shot.

During the Walker Cup matches between the United States and Great Britain and Ireland, played later in 1991 at Portmarnock, Mickleson took a leading role in his team's victory, displaying a marvellous shot-making ability.

In the third round of his successful US Amateur Championship campaign he conceded his bemused opponent a 25-foot putt for a par four at the first hole. After he had holed his own four-foot putt for a winning birdie, he commented: 'I wanted to put some pressure on myself.'

Right: *Even the big occasions don't seem to disrupt his rhythm – Mickleson at the 1991 Masters.*

A sparkling junior and amateur career preceded Colin Montgomerie's entry into the professional ranks.

Colin Montgomerie

After junior successes in the west of Scotland, where his father is club secretary at Royal Troon, Colin Montgomerie won a golf scholarship to an American university and put a sharp edge on his game in the highly competitive atmosphere. He won the Scottish Strokeplay Championship and the Scottish Amateur and was twice selected for the Walker Cup and Eisenhower Trophy teams before turning professional and winning his tour card at the qualifying school in 1987.

Although a tour victory eluded him in his first season, he was a clear winner of the Rookie of the Year award and won his place in the Scottish team for both the Dunhill and World Cup events.

His breakthrough into the winner's circle came early in the 1990 season in dramatic and emphatic fashion at the Portuguese Open. He set a new record for the Quinta do Lago course with a 63 in his final round, for a 24-under-par total and victory by no less then 11 shots over Europe's finest players.

Although he improved his order of merit standing to 14th place with £179 000 of prize-money in 1990, Montgomerie failed to add to his tally of victories, but by winning the Scandinavian Masters just one month before the Ryder Cup deadline in 1991 he secured his place in the team in style.

In his opening foursomes match with fellow team-newcomer David Gilford, he suffered defeat at the hands of Hale Irwin and Lanny Wadkins and then had to sit on the sidelines until called into action on the second afternoon, this time in successful partnership with Bernhard Langer. But he saved the high drama until the end. Five down to Mark Calcavecchia at one stage of the match, and four down with four to play, the big-hitting Scot stunned television audiences around the world by winning all four to square the match.

A player with those fighting qualities is destined for the game's dizzy heights.

Right: *Montgomerie won a Ryder Cup place in 1991 where his tenacity earned him a famous tie with Mark Calcavecchia in his singles match.*

Brett Ogle

Some golfing champions play good golf all the time and special golf when it matters most. Others can have a spectacular run for a few weeks and then go suddenly off the boil. Brett Ogle, a tall and very slim Australian, comes in the latter category.

At the start of his third year on the European tour, he warmed up with three solid top 20 performances before opening up a three-shot lead to win the AGF Open at Montpellier in southern France with the help of a second round 66. Three weeks later he shattered the course record set by Seve Ballesteros at Puerta de Hierro with an incredible final round of 61 to jump into third place in the Madrid Open.

Two weeks later he pulled out of the Benson and Hedges International half way through the second round after losing four balls on the way to a nine-over-par score. Although he apologised to his partners and left with their blessing, he had broken a PGA Tour rule and was fined.

Yet within weeks he was back in the low-scoring business again with rounds of 65, 66 and 63 for high finishes in the Dunhill Masters, the Epson Grand Prix and the European Open. In the overall performance statistics collected at every event on the tour he proved to be the fifth longest

A record-smashing 61 brought Brett Ogle third place in the 1990 Madrid Open.

With his distance and accuracy, Ogle will surely win an important tournament before long.

José Maria Olazabal

hitter, but more significantly he was also in the top 20 for greens hit in regulation, sand saves and putts.

When he left the European scene at the end of that season he collected the Australian PGA title to add to an impressive list of five other events he has won in Australia and the Far East. His 1991 progress was hampered by a broken knee-bone, a self-inflicted wound caused when a two-iron shot rebounded into him from a tree.

Brett Ogle may not be the most consistent golfer in the world, but he has the uncanny knack of scoring ultra-low tournament-winning rounds.

To put the talented Spaniard in the category of stars of the 'future' may seem like an insult. In reality José Maria Olazabal is a star of today and will be a superstar of tomorrow.

From the age of 18 he started to win almost everything he entered in Europe: two Spanish Amateur titles, plus the Italian and the British, plus the Belgian International Youths and the Boys and Youths championships in Britain. He turned professional in 1985, a year before his 20th birthday, and immediately won the six-round qualifying school.

No other player got close to the Rookie of the Year award in his first season, for he leapt

Not an easy shot for José Maria Olazabal as he plays out of water at the 15th during the 1989 Spanish Open.

Tenerife Open, 1989: Olazabal the champion is congratulated by Mark Roe (left) at the end of the final round.

straight to second place in the order of merit behind fellow Spaniard Seve Ballesteros with more than £150000 in winnings from two tournament victories and a string of high finishes. The following year was something of an anti-climax – no victories and only 17th place in the final standings, but he has since never been lower than third and has added nine more tournament wins in Europe.

His Ryder Cup record is second to none. He has formed a formidable partnership with Ballesteros for the foursomes and fourball matches and in the 1991 encounter at Kiawah Island in South Carolina they won three and a half points from a possible four. Olazabal has played three times in these encounters, taking part in every match each time. In 15 matches he has won 10, lost three and halved two.

He has also had spectacular victories outside Europe, successfully defending his Japanese Masters title with a five-stroke margin in 1990 and demolishing the field in the American World Series of Golf with a stunning 12-shot lead.

He has, more than once, come close to winning one of the four grand slam events – he finished second to Ian Woosnam in the 1991 Masters – and it cannot be long before he makes the breakthrough to win his first major.

An awkward stance for this bunker shot has Olazabal almost on his knees.

The young Spaniard demonstrates his formidable power.

Steven Richardson

The son of a St Andrews professional, Steven Richardson was born and brought up in Hampshire and captured the English Amateur Championship in 1989. At the end of that season he turned professional but could finish no higher than 36th place in the tour qualifying school.

This lower than expected placing was soon forgotten when, after an early season car crash, he had three top five placings on the Safari circuit in his first outings as a pro. He followed up with a string of 10 results in the top 25, headed by sixth place in the Desert Classic.

In the final event of his first season, the Volvo Masters over the demanding Valderrama course, he birdied the final hole to tie Sam Torrance for second place, just one stroke behind Mike Harwood. With a total of £110 000 in official prize-money it was a dream debut, which would have been crowned by nomination for Sir Henry Cotton's Rookie of the Year award, but he was just beaten to that honour by fellow newcomer Russell Claydon.

There could have been no more emphatic start to his second year among the professionals as he won the opening event of the season, the

Steven Richardson had a good start in golf – his father was a St Andrews professional.

Below: *In the 1991 US PGA Richardson came fifth, a very creditable result in a fine year.*

Girona Open, and confirmed his form with an incredible run of top 10 successes, including a second victory, the Portuguese Open, only the fifth event of the year.

Almost before the rest of Europe's pros had come out of the starting blocks, Richardson had clinched a coveted place in the European Ryder Cup team. In his baptism of fire he partnered Mark James to two excellent points in the fourball matches, but they lost their foursomes on the second day and Corey Pavin denied him success in the singles.

But an excellent fifth place in the US PGA Championship, a place in England's Dunhill Cup team and an invitation to the World Matchplay Championship, all indicated that his career was still headed sharply upwards.

Right: *Richardson had already clinched his Ryder Cup place in 1991 when some had hardly begun the season.*

Eduardo Romero

It has taken a long time for the man they call 'El Gato' – the cat – to make his mark in world golf. Although he started winning major events in his home country of Argentina back in 1983, his first attempt at the European tour in 1985 produced less than £13000 in prize-money and he had to go back to the qualifying school before he returned for a second attempt in 1988.

Again the progress was unspectacular – though more encouraging, with 48th place in the order of merit and £52000 in the bank to show for his efforts. It was a solid base to work from in the following season. In 1989 he finished fifth in an American event on his way to Europe and took sixth place in the Scottish Open before finishing with a great round of 67 in the Open Championship at Royal Troon to share eighth place with Paul Azinger and Payne Stewart.

In the Lancôme Trophy in Paris he had a spectacular run of 69, 65, 66, 66 to win his first European title by one shot from Bernhard Langer and José Maria Olazabal in a very strong field which included Greg Norman and Curtis Strange.

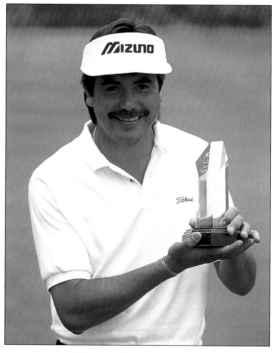

Argentinian Eduardo Romero has not made the same spectacular impact on the professional game as some of his contemporaries . . .

By the season's end he had claimed 13th place in the rankings with winnings of £183000.

This was a position he consolidated in 1990,

. . . yet his steady progress augurs well for the future. He is now achieving regular high positions on tour.

moving up a couple of places and taking his earnings over the £200000 barrier. He also confirmed his status as a tournament winner, taking the Firenze Open with another sparkling run of rounds in the 60s. He finished with four birdies in the last five holes to take the title from Colin Montgomerie.

The 1991 season brought two tour victories in an eight-week spell. In the Spanish Open he holed a 35-foot putt on the final green to tie Seve Ballesteros, five shots clear of the field. In the play-off they parred the first six holes, but Romero broke the deadlock with a superb pitch and five-foot putt for the title. Things were a little easier in the French Open where he went into the final day with a four-stroke lead and coasted home ahead of José Maria Olazabal, Sam Torrance and Nick Faldo.

Vijay Singh

There was not much depth of golfing knowledge or experience to call on for a Fijian of Indian descent, but Vijay Singh caddied for his father and showed great natural talent when he took to the game himself. There were, however, no easy stepping stones to bigger and tougher competition on his home territory.

He attempted to win his tour card to play the European circuit in 1987, but was unsuccessful and turned his talents to the African Safari circuit. He was enthusiastically supported by the Africans as he won in Nigeria and finished third in Zimbabwe and Kenya to top the Safari order of merit. Later in the season he also won the Swedish PGA Championship.

With a successful season behind him he returned to the qualifying school for the full European tour and scored six rounds over La Manga's two courses in Spain without going over par. This put him in joint second place and he was set to take the next step up the competitive ladder.

He returned to the Safari circuit where he dominated the action with victories in Zimbabwe, Nigeria and the Gold Coast, topping the money list with £40 000. This proved a fine launching pad for his first full year in Europe. He played in 32 events, winning prize-money in 21 and finishing in the top 10 five times.

More importantly he became a tournament winner in his first season, following an opening 72 with three 68s to take the Volvo Open title in Sardinia by three shots. By the season's end he had climbed to 24th place in the order of merit with £112 000 in prize-money.

In 1990 he halved his place in the rankings to 13th and almost doubled his haul of prizes to £212 000, winning the El Bosque Open on the way and again finishing in the top 10 five times. Two other performances that season gave a hint of the tremendous talent of the 6ft 2in big-hitter. He closed with a superb 65 to edge ahead of Bernhard Langer and Fred Couples into second place in the PLM Open in Sweden, and his eight-under-par total at St Andrews put him into 12th place in the Open Championship.

Fijian Vijay Singh combines immaculate touch on the short shots (left) with a swing (right) as long as his 6ft 3in frame.

TEACHERS

*F*OR as long as there have been golfers there have been people ready to tell them how to play better. The early professionals were those with a natural talent for the game who were mostly employed as caddies and expected to coach their wealthy employers. They would also partner them for big-money matches.

But the majority of golfers in those early days of the game merely developed their own style by watching and copying others. It is a fairly modern phenomenon for newcomers to sport to go straight into a series of lessons from the experts or study the latest video from Nick Faldo.

Harry Vardon, who set his record of six wins in the British Open between 1896 and 1914, was mainly responsible for a great change in the golf swing from a flat, round-the-body action from a crouched position to a more upright stance with the club being swung above the shoulder rather than behind it.

It attracted considerable criticism in his early days, but as he became more and more dominant so opinions began to change, until he was finally regarded as having the perfect golf swing. His great rival JH Taylor called him: 'The finest golfer that the game has ever produced.'

Vardon stood 'tall' to the ball and picked the club up quite quickly in the backswing. There was considerable flex in the left knee, but the right leg remained absolutely straight in the backswing. This allowed him to turn both his hips and shoulders fully 90 degrees so that his back faced the hole. The left arm was allowed to bend almost at right angles, and he maintained that the grip with the right hand should be relaxed at the top of the swing to allow full wrist movement. From this position he simply turned back into the ball with a tremendous release of the clubhead – he felt that he led the downswing with the clubhead – and swept the ball away. He did not take divots but clipped the ball off the top of the turf.

The Vardon grip which is used by the majority of players today, with the little finger of the right hand overlapping the index finger of the left, was not, in fact, his own invention. That distinction probably belonged to leading amateur Johnny Laidlay and certainly JH Taylor was using the grip before Vardon appeared on the scene. But as the man who used it to greatest effect it still bears his name today.

Vardon was renowned for his accuracy, particularly with the brassie and spoon, the two- and three-woods of today. With his upright action he was able to hit the ball higher than other professionals and favoured the shot which faded the ball slightly.

Tommy Armour, who emigrated from his native Scotland to become a golf professional in America, returned in 1931 to win the Open Championship at Carnoustie. He also won the US Open and PGA titles. But in addition to winning at the highest level, he had studied the great players of his day and when he wrote *How to Play Your Best Golf all the Time* it stayed at the top of the best-seller list in the United States for weeks. It was the first time a sports book had held that position.

Just as well received in Britain, it was a masterpiece of simple understatement. Confessing that he had thrown away hundreds of pages from the first draft, Armour said: 'I have retained only those moments in the swing which are significant. Those other pages portrayed refinements which would distract the reader from profitable concentration on essentials.'

He believed that a tight grip at address would inevitably lead to slackening at the top of the swing and a loss of control over the clubface. Good footwork was an essential part of his teaching, with the left knee pointing behind the ball at the top of the backswing and the right knee moving fast into the downswing.

If the grip on the club was firm with the last three fingers of the left hand, Armour felt that he could then let the left arm guide the club while he hit through as hard as possible with the right hand.

Another champion who believed in the importance of hand action in the swing was Henry Cotton. In later years he would encourage pupils to hit car tyres with the head of the club in an effort to build up strong wrists and increase clubhead speed.

His theory was that the left thumb acted as a sort of springboard at the top of the backswing, limiting the position of the club at the top and launching it into the downswing. At the same time, the right wrist should be relaxed to encourage good hand action at the ball.

Cotton encouraged the feeling that the hands really whipped through the ball, the back of the left hand facing the ground just after impact. He taught many pupils to hit the ball one-handed – a dozen with the right hand and a dozen with the left, repeated over and over – to build up finger and hand strength, while another of his exercises was to swing the clubhead through thick rough.

An Australian who made a big teaching impact in Britain was the former rugby league international Bill Shankland. A strict disciplinarian,

Sir Henry Cotton believed in the importance of strong hand action in the golf swing.

John Jacobs became known as Dr Golf in the 1960s. His impact on the game went far deeper than almost any other teacher of his era.

Willie Hoffmann, long-standing coach to Bernhard Langer.

Nick Faldo hard at work with his US-based coach David Leadbetter.

Coach Leadbetter – his complete remodelling of Faldo's swing brought him to the attention of the golfing public.

he put Tony Jacklin through his paces when he first joined the professional ranks and played an important part in developing his game.

An all-round athlete, Shankland instilled a natural feeling of rhythm and balance into his pupils. He very much opposed the trend to address the ball with the right shoulder in an exaggerated inside position, which, he reasoned, blocked out the use of the hands and arms in the downswing. In the hitting area he stressed the need to throw the hands as far to the left as possible. Assuming the pin was at 12 o'clock, he felt the hands should be swung to an 11 o'clock position.

In the sixties John Jacobs acquired the name 'Dr Golf' and was at the forefront in developing driving ranges with full practice facilities and par-three courses in Britain.

He followed the Tommy Armour principle in keeping his tuition as simple as possible for beginners and handicap golfers, although he spent many hundreds of hours with leading professionals who sought his advice and was appointed official coach to many national amateur teams.

He was a pioneer in making the average golfer understand the relationship between the flight of the ball and the position of the clubhead. He had an extremely quick eye and could walk along a line of a dozen pupils, giving each one a clear and simple explanation, curing a slice here and a duck hook there in a few seconds.

He made many thousands of pupils understand that if the clubface is at right angles when the ball is struck, the ball will fly straight down the line of the swing. This enables the golfer to aim his swing at the target and everything else

Left: *Bob Torrance, one of the top British coaches, gives Roger Chapman some expert guidance.*

José Maria Olazabal practising with his long-time coach Jesus Arruti.

begins to fall into place. The correct grip to get the clubface square at impact was always the starting point.

The most talked about and sought after teacher of recent times has been David Leadbetter, the English professional whom Nick Faldo found giving lessons in Florida. The two-year trans- formation of Faldo's swing was the springboard to fame for Leadbetter, who now gives advice to dozens of the world's leading tournament players.

He works on a one-to-one basis with all these players, devising routines to eliminate specific errors that may have crept into their games. In general terms he finds the average golfer often has

a poor grip, with the club clamped right in the palm of the left hand instead of lying across the base of the fingers.

Another area where club golfers get caught out is in their lack of rhythm. This often stems from a very rigid set-up position where it is difficult to get the clubhead into smooth motion. Practising with an exaggerated forward swing of the clubhead can break the tension.

There have been many excellent teachers through the years and there are club professionals all over the world who are well qualified to help any golfer improve the way they play the game. Only a few catch the headlines.

CADDIES

HOVERING in the background on every green at a golf tournament as the pros hole out, are their caddies; men – and, increasingly, women – who carry the bag and ensure the clubs are kept clean. Over the years many of them have become characters in their own right, recognised by regular golf-watchers and often referred to by television commentators.

Arnold Palmer's caddy, 'Tip' Anderson, was with him for three decades; 'Wobbly', otherwise Phil Morbey, has been with Ian Woosnam since 1987; and Nick Faldo has teamed up with Fanny Sunesson, one of a growing number of female caddies on the European tour.

Some of the younger golfers have their touring wives or girlfriends as caddies, thus saving money and enjoying their company at the same time – touring can be very lonely. Despite this trend, though, which has seen golf trolleys allowed on major courses as the ladies prefer to pull a trolley rather than carry a heavy bag, there are a fairly large number of full-time, professional caddies.

Caddies were first employed in the earliest days of golf and each golfer had more than one. There was the club-carrier, who walked round with the gentleman golfer, handing him whichever club he desired and fashioning tees for the golfer from a pocketful of wet sand; and the fore-caddy, or cadet, who would run ahead of the group of golfers and shout 'Fore!' to warn the public that a ball might be heading their way, this being in the times when golf was played over the public links, which were used by strolling couples, children and a large number of grazing sheep.

Times have, of course, changed and the caddies of today are a far cry from their predecessors, giving advice to their professionals and often travelling round the world with them. Many of the top golfers this century began their golfing 'careers' as caddies at their local clubs, including JH Taylor, Bobby Jones and, more recently, Seve Ballesteros.

Sadly the more regular use of trolleys and golf carts has meant that caddies are rarely used at golf clubs for ordinary club players these days, robbing a whole generation of young boys and girls of the opportunity to gain an interest in golf, though perhaps they now have other diversions to occupy them.

A brief moment of rest for this caddy as the players putt out.

For the caddies on the European or American tours, life is, like their employers', one long journey round from tournament to tournament, though in reality it is only the top level of caddies working regularly for one professional who find it worth their while travelling. There is an unofficial 'pool' of caddies who, present at most tournaments, always find work with one golfer. Relatively few professionals employ a full-time caddy.

In many parts of the United States and in Europe, local, experienced caddies are available for hire on a weekly basis, working for a different professional whenever there is a tournament in their area. Only the most experienced get to carry what they regard as a 'top bag' for one of the internationally acclaimed stars.

For a caddie who works regularly with one professional, the week begins on Monday morning with a flight or drive to whichever course is hosting that week's tournament. The really important luggage – the professional's golf clubs – is well looked after, having been transported in special, protective flight-bags.

Arrival at the course by midday Monday is the target, in order to get a locker in the locker-room – these are not reserved in advance and it tends to be a matter of first-come-first-served.

The clubs are then checked and cleaned, and might be re-gripped if they need it – most tournament professionals re-grip several times a season – before being safely locked away until the professional's arrival on Tuesday for a practice round. Monday evening is the time to walk the course, noting any particular landmarks to be used for yardages and any changes to the course since the last visit, probably a year before.

Tuesday is practice day and can well be a long one, with time spent on the putting green and practice range as well as on the course itself. Wednesday is traditionally pro-am day for those professionals invited to take part, the others often going to nearby courses to spend more time working on their game.

Thursday and Friday are tournament days, the early starters on Thursday teeing off at around 7.15 am, so the caddy needs to be at the course just after 6 am with the clubs, ready for the pro to get some practice in before heading for the first tee.

This is 'panic time' for the caddy, checking

Before a tournament begins the caddy will measure part of the course, making careful notes – especially on an unfamiliar course.

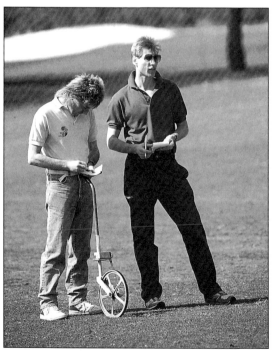

Caddies will walk the course, noting the terrain as well as distances.

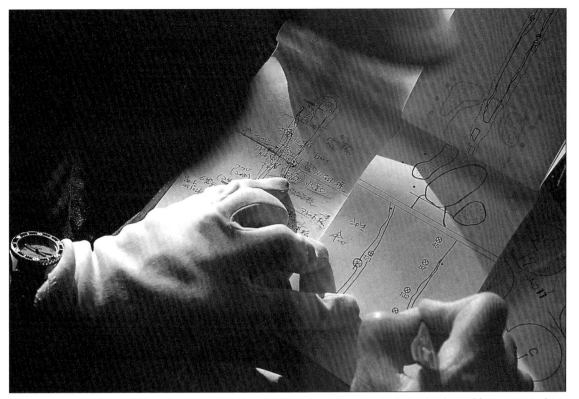

Not an ancient form of hieroglyphics – this is what is written in those little books the caddy carries in his pocket.

and re-checking that there are only 14 clubs in the bag, four or five gloves, a dozen golf balls, two sets of wet-weather clothing, towels, drinks, fruit, chocolate, biscuits or whatever else the pro might like to sustain him on his way round, and, of course, the yardage chart, suitably marked up that morning with precise pin positions for all 18 greens.

Each professional has his own characteristics. Some like to talk a lot with their caddies, others are contemplative and quiet. Some ask a lot of advice from their caddies, others don't.

Normally, according to Paul Ray, an English caddy who has spent four years on the European tour, the pro will ask for exact distances to the pin and the amount of space between the flag and the back of the green (nobody likes to go through the back!), and will often ask for reassurance as to which club he should use.

'The golfer wants to know what club he can use to safely reach the pin, depending on the conditions and what hazards there are in the way. Some are very relaxed when they hit a bad shot; others need to have their concentration re-set regularly as they can be distracted by everything

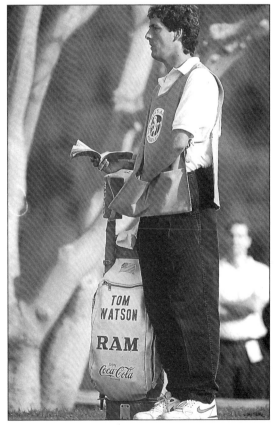

Tom Watson's caddy checks yardages to give his player the exact distance to the flag.

going on around them. It is teamwork, and personalities count for a great deal.'

Once on the green the caddy might be consulted about the line of a putt or the break of the green, but the last word is always with 'the boss'. He, after all, is the one hitting the ball.

The flag must be held and should not touch the green to show the line of a putt; the bag must be laid well off the green so that it is not in the line of any ball.

At the end of the round the professional will usually spend several more hours practising, during which time the caddy is on hand to keep the clubs clean. At the end of the day – often into early evening – it's time to lock the clubs away ready for the second round on Friday. If the player makes the 'cut' on Friday night, Saturday and Sunday are the same before it is time to pack up and travel early on Monday morning.

Most caddies work for a pre-agreed weekly

A long walk with a heavy bag – and that's just part of the day.

The distance estimated, the club chosen – now it's up to the player.

Left: *Greg Norman shares a joke with caddy Pete Bender during the 1986 Open at Turnberry.*

Seve Ballesteros' caddy helps with the line of a putt.

wage and take a percentage of the winnings, ranging from 5% for a place outside the top ten to 10% for a win. A top-ten finish other than first normally brings about 7.5%, so a good week could bring the caddy a few thousand pounds, though they are not as common as either the caddies or the professionals would like! More often than not, after the flights, hotels and meals have been paid for – and most caddies live cheaply, sharing rooms whenever possible and eating frugally – there is little left over for a rainy day.

Only for experienced caddies on the top bags can the profession pay handsomely, one top player's caddy living in some luxury and earning more than enough to pay cash for a Porsche 944. This is the exception rather than the rule, however. Caddies for 'top bags' also receive money from sponsors and can earn anything up to £50000 a year. The vast majority are happy just to break even.

Becoming a caddy takes some perseverance. It is not just a matter of turning up at a golf tournament and offering to carry a bag, yet ironically that is how many of today's caddies began their careers.

Anyone seriously contemplating caddying would be well advised to offer their services at a regional or local professional or amateur tournament to gain experience before venturing to offer their services to a touring professional. That is how Paul Ray began, by asking Ian Moseley if he could carry his bag at a pro-am at Wentworth. He has since carried for Eamonn Darcy and several other European tour pros.

Experience at these lower levels would be highly valued when the time comes to apply to join the big league. There is, in Europe, the European Tour Caddies Association, which helps to look after the interests of its members and to ensure they conform to the highest standards. The United States has a similar body but with stricter conditions. On the US tour every professional must use a qualified, recognised caddy. Wives and girlfriends, unless they are qualified caddies, just will not do.

In the Far East and Japan, however, female

Praying it's the right club! Many caddies on tour are fine players themselves, so their knowledge can be of real assistance to their professional.

caddies are the rule rather than the exception, even at professional tournaments. Apart from a few visiting professionals from America or Australia, most of the caddies on the Asian tour are females, and very protective of the professionals for whom they carry.

The life of the full-time caddy has changed radically over the years, since the 1940s. Then, and until relatively recently, caddies were not allowed in the clubhouse, being relegated well below the salt. Today, though, the established ones are often personalities in their own right. For them, and the top golfers they carry for, teamwork means just that.

Jack Nicklaus decides which club to use, advised by long-serving caddy Jimmy Dickinson.

SPONSORSHIP

*A*PART from being an enjoyable game to watch and play, golf has now become a multi-million-pound business. Television has been largely responsible for popularising the sport, with its regular coverage of major events.

That coverage, in turn, has given many companies the opportunity to have their brand names almost subliminally presented to a wide audience, via sponsorship of top players. Company names and brand logos now appear on golf bags, players' shirts and sun visors, and in the background on hoardings and scoreboards. One company recently estimated the coverage it gained from having its logo on a top player's sun visor during the US Open was worth over $2 million – what it would have had to pay in advertising to get the same amount of TV time for its product. The company pays the professional $6.5 million over a ten-year period.

Golf is not, of course, the only sport to gain from such sponsorship. In the UK, football, Grand Prix racing and horse racing receive even more money than golf. Yet between them, these four sports, perhaps because of their highly visual image thanks to television, receive the bulk of the estimated £400 million spent each year on sports sponsorship. In the United States the figures are even higher, baseball, basketball and gridiron football all being eager recipients of vast sums of sponsors' money.

Sponsorship in golf is nothing new, of course, with deals going back to 1900 when Harry Vardon, having then won three British Opens, set off on a 26 000-mile tour of the United States – by

Harry Vardon was one of the first golfers to gain sponsorship, in 1900.

Corporate hospitality involves five-star service in a marquee – and is vital to the financial success of a tour event.

Left: *Sponsorship means teaching the boss! Nick Faldo gives some advice to Masato Mizuno, managing director of the club manufacturer.*

train in those days – to promote a new golf ball named after him. He was paid to play exhibition matches with the new ball and travelling salesmen from the manufacturers accompanied him to sell the ball wherever they went.

For Vardon it was financially worthwhile, even though it left him physically exhausted and suffering from tuberculosis. The ball itself was not a success, being replaced in the march of technological progress.

Other deals followed and several of the early 'greats' of golf found companies ready and willing to offer them decent sums of money to add their name or endorsement to a variety of products. With little prize-money then on offer, it is hardly surprising that few such offers were turned down.

Sponsorship has continued right down the ages since then, though only recently has it

Right: *Volvo's sponsorship of the European Tour means a high profile for the car manufacturer, while its involvement in golf has been a major factor in the Tour's success.*

become such big business. Back in 1945, Byron Nelson, having just won 11 professional tournaments on the trot, was given $200 to appear as a cartoon character on a cereal packet. Such a winning streak these days would probably result in a deal closer to $2 million.

It was as recently as the 1960s that Arnold Palmer, having won two British Open championships (1961 and 1962), was persuaded by an entrepreneurial young lawyer to let him manage the golf star's off-course financial affairs. The young man, Mark McCormack, then signed up the young Jack Nicklaus and Gary Player, having a 'stable' of the three top golfers in the world.

With the expansion of television coverage of golf, together with the clean image the sport had – and still enjoys – sponsors were easily found who were willing to part with a few hundred thousand dollars to have Mr Palmer wear their logo on his shirts. Wilson, the golf club manufacturer, parted equally happily with similar amounts to have the great man use their clubs and have their name on his bag.

Yet even by the mid-seventies few golfers were receiving much money from sponsors – Jerry Pate, a US Amateur champion in 1974 before turning professional, was signed up by Wilson for just $7500, though he did receive a further $10 000 bonus from the company for winning the 1976 US Open.

It was just after this that sponsorship began to take off in a big way, though not led by Palmer, Nicklaus and Player but by another McCormack protegé, Australian Greg Norman.

His white-haired, clean image, together with his aggressive style and playing ability, so impressed would-be sponsors that they were happy to pile millions of dollars into his bank account; so much so that by 1990 he was reputedly earning $8 million a year from 27 different sponsors (including such non-golf names as Hertz and McDonald's) without even hitting a golf ball. For hitting the right type of ball – a Maxfli – he is paid a further $1 million over five years.

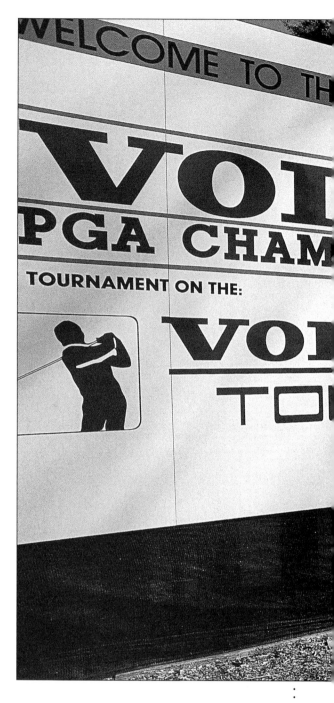

Palmer, however, at 62 years of age, still edges ahead with $9 million, supplemented by his other businesses which include six car dealerships and a golf course development company.

Nicklaus, too, makes over $7 million from sponsorship, to add to his income from a shareholding in the MacGregor club manufacturing business, his golf course design company (at a minimum $1 million per course) and other investments, though he is no longer with the McCormack organisation.

Other US golfers, including Lee Trevino,

Payne Stewart, Curtis Strange, Tom Watson and Ray Floyd, have all easily topped a million dollars a year in sponsorship deals, so much so that there are few players in the US top 20 money-winners who are not dollar millionaires.

In Europe, too, sponsorship has risen dramatically over the past decade, with Spain's Severiano Ballesteros being the first and most successful player to tug at the purse-strings of major sponsors. It is now not just golf equipment manufacturers which pay to benefit from Seve's endorsement, but clothing manufacturers and even a parfumier. Seve, too, has his own golf course design company and has been involved in some course and residential developments.

Nick Faldo, also a McCormack (through his company, IMG) client, has signed some highly publicised deals with Mizuno, the Japanese club manufacturer, and Pringle, the clothing supplier. Both deals are based on royalties of the products sold over a five-year period and both are estimated at £5 million, though IMG denies there is a firm figure – it could be even more than that! Faldo is also reported to have been paid £1 million by Bic razors in 1990.

The amount each company spends on sponsorship is normally a well-guarded secret, though Dunlop/Slazenger does admit that 40% of its entire golf promotional budget, which includes advertising and PR, is spent on direct sponsorship of players. Any player winning a major like the British Open or the US Masters virtually leaps instantly into the millionaire class, if he is not there already.

Even promising young first-year professionals can find sponsors willing to invest up to about

Charities benefit from golf, too. A substantial amount each year finds its way to good causes. Here Nick Faldo hands over another sizeable cheque.

£30000 in them, plus endless supplies of clubs, balls and clothes. To be fair, it costs a minimum of £30000 to spend a year on the European tour these days, with travel, hotels, caddies and other living expenses. The need for some money to put by creates the desire to do well on the course – even a player coming 20th these days is likely to receive around £5000 – and there is a need to earn enough in prize-money to qualify to stay on the tour, only the top 120 automatically qualifying each year. Sponsors cannot be expected to back a loser for too long!

The growing amount of prize-money on the tour – the European tour now has prize-money in excess of £16 million a season – has made it easier for more professionals to make a good living. In the US, too, prize-money is such that winning is no longer financially necessary; several weeks of coming in the top 30 are all that is needed to live comfortably, the day-to-day expenses coming from eager sponsors, cultivated by clever management groups.

Sponsors of golf tournaments, like insurance giant GA, Lufthansa, Bell's and Heineken in Europe and many others in the United States and elsewhere, do, of course, like to see the top players at their event, for that helps to guarantee better television coverage and a large number of spectators through the gates. From this has come the only serious bone of contention in golf – appearance money.

The top players – like Ballesteros, Faldo, Woosnam, Stewart, Strange, Watson, Norman and others – are often guaranteed huge amounts, sometimes in excess of the winner's official prize-money, just to turn up and play. One leading international player arriving at a European Championship a couple of years ago was guaranteed $200000. The first prize was only $140000. In the event that player failed to make the cut and went home on the Friday night flight.

Not all professionals are so mercenary, or perhaps are not in a position to be so. Most of them try to do well to please the sponsors, the public and, presumably, themselves, for no one likes to play badly. Some, of course, just refuse to play without a large injection of dollars into their bank accounts. Whilst no one will comment officially on appearance money a figure of around £40000 is

	TOURNAMENTS PLAYED	ROUNDS PLAYED	STROKE AVERAGE
1. PARRY	5	20	70·90
2 RICHARDSON	11	40	70·97
3 OLAZABAL	7	28	71·21
4 MARTIN	9	31	71·39
5 BALLESTEROS	3	10	71·60
6 SINGH	9	36	71·61
7 FEHERTY	9	31	71·65
8 LANGER	3	9	71·67
9 HOAD	2	8	71·75
10 WHELAN	9	15	71·80
11 TORRANCE	10	36	71·97
12 McLEAN	10	40	72·12
13 LANNER	8	26	72·19
14 BOSSERT	3	10	72·20
15 WOOSNAM	3	10	72·30
16 ROMERO	9	32	72·34
17 CALI	9	32	72·34
18 ROE	9	29	72·41
19 ROCCA	10	38	72·45
20 LANE	8	28	72·50

0898 168 165 The official service to the PGA EUROPEAN TOUR

William HILL FIRST AGAIN

Every round played is vital, as the averages here show – money is on offer here, too, not just to tournament winners.

believed to be common for a top player. For that, the sponsors hope to increase the 'gate' and sell more television coverage around the world.

It happens in other sports too, of course, and players can hardly be expected to turn down a good offer. The only major areas of contention are the relatively few times a player does not try his best and the times when a player misses a major tour event to play in an exhibition match elsewhere.

For lesser-known professionals, though – and that is the vast majority of them – sponsorship is the only way they can manage to play professional golf. In their early years on tour they could never win enough to stay alive, so the sponsorship money is a necessary investment in their future by companies which believe they will gain sufficient long-term coverage to make it worthwhile.

Since many company chairmen are also keen amateur golfers there is an element of self-interest too, though that is not unlike political or charitable donations elsewhere. And without a sufficient number of quality, professional golfers, there would be nobody for Ballesteros, Norman, Faldo and Stewart to beat!

MANAGING A GOLF STAR

SINCE Mark McCormack signed up the young Arnold Palmer in 1960, golfers, like other leading sportsmen and women, have left their financial and other affairs to teams of managers, allowing them to do what they enjoy most – play golf.

All the top golfers, and many further down the list, have managers, either large groups like IMG or individual managers, who look after their affairs and maybe those of just a couple of other golfers.

Whilst Palmer, Norman, Woosnam and Faldo are all IMG clients, not every top golfer is with the largest management group in the world. Seve Ballesteros, for example, was, until recently, managed by his brother, thus keeping all the earnings in the family.

Christy O'Connor Jnr is managed by a friend in Ireland; another young Irishman, Darren Clarke, is managed by an ex-European tour player turned manager, Andrew Chandler, whose other clients include Richard Boxall, Carl Mason and Deryk Cooper.

The financial details vary from player to player, but basically the manager or management group takes 25% of all sponsorship deals together with 10% of on-course winnings. For this the player has all the details of his day-to-day life taken away, leaving him to do nothing more strenuous than play golf. And at the top level that is, in itself, a full-time job.

When one considers what a golfer's life entails, it is, for most players, well worth the money, even if, in Palmer's case, it means IMG earning over $2 million a year for managing his sponsorship deals. Certainly, McCormack has advanced the popularity of golf by attracting vast amounts of money into the game, as well as spreading it around to a larger number of players.

Colin Montgomerie, the Scot, is a typical IMG client. He began his professional career in 1987 and was signed by IMG in 1989. Sponsors were found which included Pringle, Wilson and

Mark McCormack of IMG, the world's largest management group.

the Gleneagles Hotel, giving Colin enough off-course money to guarantee him a decent living for three years. Taking away the worry over the financial side of life allowed him to concentrate on golf. In 1991 he won the Scandinavian Masters, one of the richest events on the European tour. That victory earned him £100 000 and helped him achieve a Ryder Cup place, playing in Kiawah Island for Great Britain and Europe. That success on the course has now added to his 'sales potential' off it and further sponsorship deals can be expected to follow.

IMG handles his financial and tax matters and advises him on investments and other business affairs, as well as talking with him regularly as to which tournaments would be best for him to enter to bring some sanity to his schedule. IMG also takes care of all his travel arrangements, with airline and hotel reservations being made as necessary and payment of bills being handled as they arrive. There is an IMG office in almost every major country, so help is never far away at any time.

In return Montgomerie is expected to make certain appearances at the behest of sponsors – a company golf day, perhaps, or a dinner or drink with an important guest at a golf tournament. IMG handles all these arrangements, as well as ensuring he has sufficient foreign currency on every trip, saving that irritating wait at the airport bureau de change.

There are, of course, critics who would say the relationship is based on greed, trying to maximise the golfer's income for the benefit of IMG and of the golfer. Without doubt there is the desire to maximise income, yet this differs from no other business on earth.

What golf has not seen is the early 'burn-out' of players as they try to win everything in sight in the first couple of years, a situation which has arisen in other sports, notably ladies' tennis. Golf is less physically taxing, being more of a mind game; in such situations, emotional maturity and experience can count far more than just ability. IMG sees its relationship with the players it manages as a 'long-term partnership', with regular meetings to discuss progress.

Andrew Chandler, by contrast with the vastness of IMG, is more of a one-man band, managing a dozen golfers on what is a totally personal basis. He, too, handles tax and other matters for his clients, makes their airline and hotel reservations, gives them cash advances as necessary and takes care of all sponsorship deals.

Finding sponsors is, for him, slightly more difficult than it might be for IMG, particularly as he is a relative newcomer to the world of management. His 15 years as a European tour player do, however, give him a vast amount of experience of what today's young tour professional can expect out in what he describes as 'the minefield'. He sees his task as being to guide the younger players through that minefield, again leaving them to concentrate purely on golf.

He is normally at each golf tournament to talk with the professionals he manages, believing that being close to them is vital. Although he does not teach golf – even though eminently qualified to do so – he does also talk to them about the technical aspects of their swing and will recommend particular coaches for each player. Knowing each of the European tour courses from personal

His years as a professional golfer on tour allow Andrew Chandler (left) to help and advise those he now manages.

experience, he can also suggest which courses might best suit each player, knowing their technical strengths and weaknesses.

What he sees his job as being is to guide each of his charges towards a clearly defined goal. It is almost a career development plan, year by year, rather than an 'I want to be the best' ambition, with realistic targets which might not even include winning a tournament in the early years.

Managing a golfer is not an easy job for there is little real glamour in it for either the majority of players or their managers, and cashing in on an Arnold Palmer is about as rare as a birdie on the 17th at St Andrews.

To be worthwhile it has to be a very long-term relationship in an area where there are few written contracts between players and managers. It is a relationship built on understanding, success on both sides – getting results for the player; getting sponsors for the manager – and, perhaps most importantly, on trust.

Off-course sponsorship from several companies has allowed Colin Montgomerie to concentrate on winning at golf.

THE CLUB PROFESSIONAL

MOST people's main contact with the world of professional golf – apart from seeing the major touring stars at tournaments or on television – is at the local golf club where the professional dispenses golf balls, starting times and advice.

Becoming a professional is not easy, yet there are many young men and women who want to make a career out of golf, though not all of them have either the ability or desire to take the plunge into tournament golf. For them the life of the club professional holds far more promise; there are far more club professionals than touring professionals.

For the aspiring club professional, a basic apprenticeship needs to be served before he or she can be called a professional golfer; during this

A busy club shop, where the professional is responsible for sales and green fees.

four-year period the trainee learns to teach the golf swing, to repair clubs and to run a busy golf shop – an increasingly important part of a club professional's life – as well as the rules of golf and tournament administration.

In Britain the profession is governed by the Professional Golfers' Association (PGA) based at the Belfry and it is to this body that any young person should apply, once they have decided they would like to try.

There is a six-month probationary period prior to officially becoming a trainee and this period lets the aspirant decide whether he or she likes the life. It also tells the club professional in charge whether he or she has the right attitude and aptitude for the career. At this stage amateur status is not lost, an important point for those who do not make the grade.

After that probationary period the applicant will become a registered trainee, attached to an approved teaching professional – in essence almost all of them. It is at this stage that the trainee becomes a professional and can no longer play in amateur events. There are certain basic qualifications which need to be achieved to become a trainee, including educational qualifications in Maths and English, and a playing handicap of 5 or less.

Traineeship lasts a minimum of three years and a maximum of four, and during this period the trainees must also play in local and regional tournaments against other budding professionals, giving them not only the challenge of competing against their peers but also the vital experience of preparing mentally and physically for golf tournaments, for most club professionals continue to play in tournaments – not major events like the British Open but regional or national competitions for club professionals – throughout their lives. In the four-year training period a minimum of 25 competitions must be entered and the trainee must achieve at least three scores of no worse than four over par for the four rounds.

The PGA also runs residential schools which the trainees must attend, ensuring that they are fully conversant with all aspects of golf; it also gives them an opportunity to mix with other young trainees for a vital exchange of views and ideas.

In their fourth year the trainees take a five-day examination, to check their knowledge of all aspects of golf course administration, the rules of golf, teaching, public speaking and, of course, their playing ability, which is checked over their period of traineeship and must relate to a handicap of four or better, based on the events they have played.

All subjects need to be passed before the status of full PGA professional is granted. Any subjects failed can be retaken, but only within the four-year period. After that, any who have failed will get no further opportunity to follow the route into professional golf unless their playing ability is so good that they can qualify for the European tour. Those failing at this stage can re-apply for amateur status.

Once the final examinations are passed, the trainee becomes a fully qualified PGA golf professional, yet that does not mean he or she takes over a golf club immediately. Most will need to spend at least a couple of years working as an assistant professional to gain extra experience before applying for their 'own' club position.

Taking on such a position also requires some money, or credit-worthiness, for the contents of the professional shop need to be purchased, often with an expensive bank loan. With several dozen sets of golf clubs, shoes, golf bags, balls, gloves and clothes the investment is of the order of many thousands of pounds, the average professional shop in 1991 being stocked with goods to a retail value of between £10000 and £100000.

A club professional's job is not exactly an easy one but it is most enjoyable for those dedicated enough to have chosen this particular way of life. It involves long hours including weekends, which are normally the busiest time of the week, and in the summer an early start and a late finish, most courses opening at or before 8 am and not closing until around 9 pm. The winters are, naturally, less busy.

Sales from the club shop are vital to the livelihood of a club professional, often accounting for over 50% of his income, the remainder coming from lessons to members on an individual or group basis. The growth of high street golf discount shops with their modern merchandising methods has put the club professional under enormous pressure, so much so that many club professionals have joined together in buying groups to obtain better discounts on equipment than they could if they were buying on an individual basis. They have learnt to market and sell golf equipment in a more professional manner, competing on price with the high street golf 'supermarkets'.

For a member buying a new set of clubs they can often give better advice than a high street store, for the professional has probably seen the member playing and knows the strengths and weaknesses of the swing, thus allowing exact matching of clubs to player, with the added option of being able to try out certain clubs on grass on the first tee rather than in an artificial range. Getting properly-fitted clubs is as important as buying the right size shoes.

The weekly or monthly medal competitions need to be supervised and liaison with the greenkeepers maintained to ensure the course is in tip-top condition. Then there are always club repairs, lessons and a requirement to play golf with the members from time to time, something they all enjoy, for that is the reason for taking up a professional golfer's life in the first place.

The professional is often a pivotal figure at many private clubs, solving the many little problems which inevitably arise when many people want to play golf – often all at the same time! With visiting groups and society and company days, the balance needs to be struck between the needs of the groups and those of local members who don't want to be denied access to 'their' course.

At the many municipal courses in Britain the professional is often asked to wear two hats – one as green-fee collector and starter, handing the money over to the local authority, and the other as teacher and shop manager, the last two activities providing his or her main income. Teaching at municipal courses has become far more important as this is often where beginners go to learn the game. There are, too, waiting lists for membership at most established golf clubs.

For those who have made the grade it is anything but an easy life, with long hours, particularly in summer. Yet the life can be rewarding, both financially and emotionally, when a club pro can watch a pupil steadily improve under his tutelage. That, according to many club professionals, is what it's all about.

Out in all weathers the professional teaches his pupils, passing on the benefit of his knowledge and skill.

PART THREE

COURSES

COURSE ARCHITECTURE

WHILE the true origins of the game of golf remain shrouded in the mists of antiquity, the birth of golf course architecture is a little more clearly defined and can be traced back to a period towards the end of the 19th century.

And although some might argue that the first dawning of course design happened over a hundred years earlier in 1764 when the golfers of St Andrews decided to reduce their original layout from 22 holes to 18, it is generally accepted that it was between 1896 and the start of the 1920s that the fundamentals of good course architecture were laid down.

Those 'fundamentals', many of which still hold true today, were initially drawn up by eight men; four golf professionals and four amateur players, none of whom had any previous experience in either golf course design or construction. However, what they did possess was the ability to recognise the many different elements which, when brought together through experience, imagination and careful thought, made the game so enjoyable to like-minded individuals who then, as now, stood in judgement over their labours.

In its infancy, the role of the course architect was basically to enhance that which nature had already created. As yet, architecture for architecture's sake had no role to play in the scheme of things and the models for those early designers were the famous links courses, which owed their existence more to the hand of nature than to the labours of man. In fact, inland sites were often stripped of trees, which at one time were seen as nothing more than a nuisance. Wayward golfers today might agree!

Before the turn of the century, golf course design was carried out by professional golfers, many of whom were past Open champions. Old

The old links courses were thought to be a true test of golf. The Hell Bunker on the 14th at St Andrews is certainly testing.

Tom Morris designed Dornoch, the initial course at Muirfield, the New Course at St Andrews and also Macrihanish. However, it was another Open champion, Willie Park, who first defined the attributes of a well-designed golf course.

In a chapter from his book, *The Game of Golf*, Park maintained that laying out a golf course

was a task which required great skill and judgement, and as such, should only be carried out by those who were experienced in these matters. He went on to suggest that the first tee and the last green should be close to the clubhouse, and that if the site permitted, the clubhouse should also be in a raised position giving a good outlook over the course.

With regard to how the holes should be routed, Park suggested that the first two holes should be fairly long but fairly easy to play, allowing the golfers to get off to a reasonably fast start and avoid congestion. He also advocated at least two short holes, 'within reach of the good player in one stroke'. Also, in the case of new greens, the holes should be made shorter to begin with, until the ground was 'walked down'.

Tees, Park believed, should always be placed on a level part of the course, sloping slightly upwards in the direction of the hole.

He was also a great believer in introducing variety to the design of the course through the positioning of the greens, which he felt should always be large and of a slightly undulating character. On the question of hazards, Park maintained there should never be a hazard from

A perfect setting for the golf architect: Tayaiho Golf Club, Gotemba, Japan. Mount Fuji forms the backdrop.

which the ball could not be extricated with the loss of one stroke, that all hazards should be visible to the golfer before he played his stroke and that they should never be introduced in a place where they could penalise a good shot.

Many of the early courses were, to say the least, severe tests, with savage hazards and poor playing conditions. However, the emergence of views which were more in tune with a kindly and more gentle approach to course design began to evolve; and around the turn of the century, James Taylor began to exert a strong influence on the direction which good golf course architecture should follow.

In 1902 the five-times Open champion wrote a book called *Taylor on Golf*, in which he suggested a formula for establishing a uniform length for the holes. Taylor was not a believer in what was referred to at the time as 'Sloggers' golf'. He believed that between 140 and 150 yards was the ideal length for a par three, while a par four, or two-stroke hole as it was then known, should play to between 320 and 330 yards, based on the fact that the average distance for a drive at that

South Africa has many fine courses in glorious settings. This is Sun City, home of the Million Dollar Challenge.

as Sir John Vanbrugh who, when describing landscaping work he had carried out at Castle Howard, said: 'I may commend them because Nature made them; I pretend no more merit than a midwife who helps bring a child into the world out of bushes, bogs and bryars.'

In 1903 another name came to prominence in the world of golf course design, that of John Low. A St Andrews member and captain of the Cambridge team, he published a book in 1903 called *Concerning Golf*, in which he said: 'Every fresh hole we play should teach us a further step in the progress of our golfing knowledge. Inland golf is often decried, and is certainly not so pleasant as the seaside game, but it is splendid in schooling as a supplement to the more sterling stuff. Most of the fine players of today have played much of their golf on inland greens, and have learned that the shots which are necessary on such links are often expedient on the classic courses.'

He concluded: 'The very worst greens often teach us the most, even as the worst lies, when overcome, make us the more master of every possibility of a situation.'

John Low went on to define a test of golf as follows: 'A course which necessitates power combined with great accuracy on the part of the player supplies the first principles of a good test. The course which requires, in addition to those things, the playing of the greatest variety of strokes, will be the best test of all.' He goes on to give two examples of the type of hole design he is referring to, quoting, as outstanding examples, the second holes at St Andrews and Hoylake.

In both cases the first shot must be played well to the right in order to find the best position from which to, in the author's words, 'conduct further operations'. This means that the hole must not be played as a series of isolated shots with no bearing to each other, but instead each stroke must be played in relation to the following one, and the hole approached with a preconceived plan of action.

This far-sighted concept was almost tantamount, in golfing terms, to the discovery of the

time was around the 175-yard mark. When it came to par fives, Taylor suggested that 470 yards should be the average length.

Despite the lack of specialised construction equipment, there was a tremendous increase in the growth of golf courses over the first half of the century and gradually the quality of the playing conditions improved. The hazards became a little softer and also a little less severe. Yet although new ideas and design techniques were slowly evolving, the course architects of the day, on the whole, remained true to the doctrine of men such

Bobby Jones wanted to create a course which was both testing and a source of pleasure. With the vision of Alister

Mackenzie he succeeded at Augusta.

wheel and was the kind of forward thinking which helped change the philosophy of golf course architecture, away from the traditional 'slogger' approach to that of a more skilful and tactical perception of how the game should be played.

Of hazards Low said: 'What tests good golf is the hazard which may or may not be risked; the bunker which takes charge of the long, but not quite truly-hit ball. There is hardly such a thing as an unfair bunker. Even the hazard right in the middle of the course at the end of a long tee shot, like the ninth hole bunker at St Andrews, is really quite a fair risk.'

He continued: 'Golf need not be played in bee-lines. It is a mistake to suppose that because you hit a shot straight down the middle of the course and find it bunkered you are to fill up the offending hazard. Next time you will play on the true line, not the bee-line, and all will be well. There seems to me to be far too few "round-the-corner" holes in golf.

'The greedy golfer will go too near and be sucked in to his destruction. The straight player will go just as near the hazard as he deems safe, just as close as he dare. That's golf and that's hazards of immortal importance. For golf should be a contest of risks. The fine player should just be slipping past the bunkers, gaining every yard he can, conquering by confidence of his own "far and sure" play. The less skilful player should wreck himself either by attempting risks which are beyond his skill, or by being compelled to lose ground through giving the bunkers a wide berth. Good bunkers refuse to be disregarded and insist on asserting themselves; they do not mind being avoided, but they decline to be ignored.'

Summing up his philosophy on golf course design, Low concludes: 'A perfect tee shot should make the following shot less difficult; a perfect second shot should only be probable after the perfect first. Each step of the journey should be hazardous; the links should be almost too difficult for the players.'

Almost a hundred years have passed since John Low laid out his blueprint for good golf course design, but it holds as true today as it did in 1903.

A few years later, the first real advance of the decade in golf equipment arrived, in the shape of the Haskell rubber golf ball, which all but made the gutta-percha ball obsolete overnight. Although the great James Braid, who won the 1911 British Open playing the new Haskell ball, claimed that he was four strokes a round better when playing the old gutta-percha ball, the new Haskell ball was to have a major impact on course architecture. And a man who was to play a leading role in the shaping of the future of golf course design over the next decade, and even through to the present day, was HS Colt.

A contemporary of John Low, Colt first game to prominence when he designed the Eden course at St Andrews in 1914. And the imaginative landscaping which he carried out, on what was initially a relatively flat piece of land, was to become a Colt trademark which would be repeated and often copied on many great layouts, both in Great Britain and around the world.

Colt also carried out the redesign of several major links courses, first designed by the likes of Old Tom Morris and other leading players of that time, to help defend these great courses against the advances in equipment such as the new Haskell ball.

There was a new breed of architect emerging, some of whom were gifted amateurs like Herbert Fowler who designed Walton Heath. Fowler had definite views on how the strategic aspects of golf course architecture should develop: 'The ideal course should have difficulties both in the tee and approach shot, and if possible, the hazards should be so arranged that the player having "placed" his tee shot shall play the second shot at an advantage over the player who has been wild.'

On the subject of greens, Fowler suggested that there should always be an 'entrance' to every green and that the width of that entrance should vary, depending on the distance the approach shot is played from.

HS Colt had formerly been a solicitor and also secretary at Sunningdale golf club, and was to become one of the leading lights in course architecture over the next thirty years. Writing in *The Book of the Links*, he said: 'I am sick to death of seeing so many thirty-by-thirties in greens and ten-by-tens in tees.'

Standardisation, claimed Colt, destroyed half the fun of the game. The designer should see

Medinah, Illinois, an excellent Mid-West course which hosted the 1990 US Open.

1. Two loops of nine holes are preferable.

2. At least four short holes, two or three drive-and-pitch holes and a large preponderance of good two-shot holes.

3. Short walks only from green to following tee, preferably forward to leave elasticity for future lengthening.

4. Undulating greens and fairways but no hill-climbing.

5. A different character to every hole.

6. Minimum blindness for the approach.

7. Beautiful surroundings and man-made features, indistinguishable from nature.

8. Sufficient heroic carries from the tee but alternative routes for the shorter player if he sacrifices a stroke or a half-stroke.

9. Endless variety in shot-making.

10. No lost balls.

11. Playing interest to stimulate improvement in performance.

12. High-scoring golfers should still be able to enjoy the layout.

13. Perfect greens and fairways, approaches equal to greens and conditions just as good in winter as in summer.

and then use the natural features on each course to the fullest possible extent. The more natural the hazards on a course, whatever their character, the more interesting the course ought to be.

All of which agreed with James Braid's beliefs as published in *Advanced Golf* in 1908: 'Every natural obstacle [is] to be used and there should be complete variety of holes in length and character and design. Putting greens should always be well guarded and the shorter the hole, the smaller the green should be. There should also be alternative tees and bunkering for positional play as well as alternative routes.'

By now the demand for new golf courses was starting to gather momentum and certain criteria were evolving with regard to such things as length of holes, landscape of fairways and artificial mounding to enhance the natural contours of the site.

In 1920, Colt went into partnership with Dr Alister Mackenzie who produced a 13-point plan for the ideal golf course:

Dr Alister Mackenzie was to become one of the most respected and influential golf course architects in the world and these 13 principles are clearly evident in all his work, nowhere more so than at the Augusta National course in Georgia, home of the famous US Masters and perhaps the most beautiful and best strategically-designed inland golf course in the world.

Another fine example of Mackenzie's work can be found at the magnificent Alwoodley course a few miles north of the city of Leeds. Set among some of the finest golfing land in Yorkshire, here you will discover 18 superb holes, each with its own character and design, offering an exciting challenge to both the golfer's skill and imagination.

In a remarkably short span of time between the turn of the century and the late 1920s, most of the basic criteria for good golf course architecture were clearly established and the only real advancements in course design since then have been of a mechanical nature, as the result of more powerful and sophisticated earth-moving machinery.

The period between the two world wars has been described as the golden age of golf course architecture, with men like Colt, Mackenzie and Donald Ross designing masterpieces that are still unsurpassed today.

In the late forties and early fifties the advances in construction techniques meant that even the most unattractive sites could be shaped and fashioned into whatever concept the architect had in mind. Today it is possible to build a course on an old rubbish tip; and in Japan, where land is at a premium, even mountain tops have been removed to provide a workable site.

Such powerful tools can, however, sometimes tempt a designer to completely ignore the natural features of a site and attempt to impose his will totally on the land. The end result of such efforts is often not only totally alien to its surroundings but can also be difficult to maintain in good order.

One of the leading lights of the modern generation of golf course designers is an American, Robert Trent Jones. Involved from the start in the concept and design of the resort golf course, Jones was often under pressure in the early days to produce the best possible course in the shortest time and for the least amount of money. Yet despite these pressures, Trent Jones has designed many excellent courses throughout the world.

If the likes of Colt, Mackenzie and Ross were responsible for what might be described as the 'Renaissance' period in golf course architecture, then Tom Fazio and Pete Dye represent the 'Impressionist' school of course design. Pete Dye, in particular, has gained a reputation for being adventurous, sometimes in the extreme. Yet like many of his great counterparts of the 1920s and 1930s, he always strives to incorporate his ideas into the natural surroundings of the site and, whenever possible, to work in harmony with the existing contours of the surrounding landscape.

Today, golf course design has come almost full circle as we now see many of the great players of the modern era following the example of Old Tom Morris, James Braid, Harry Vardon and JH Taylor by becoming architects. Names such as Arnold Palmer, Johnny Miller and Tom Weiskopf are all heavily associated with designing courses, with Jack Nicklaus, the most successful golfer of modern times, also claiming the title of 'most prolific architect' with literally dozens of his courses under construction all over the world.

Modern-day course architecture is a multi-million-dollar business which now enlists the aid of powerful computers with specially created software packages that can simulate almost every aspect of a golf course, from the way the growth of new trees will affect the shape of a hole in ten years' time, to producing almost exact copies of some of the game's most famous bunkers. And all before a single spadeful of soil is disturbed!

Yet despite the computers and the powerful, modern earth-moving equipment, the fundamentals of golf course design remain the same as they were a hundred years ago, as do the requirements for the ideal site on which to build an 18-hole course. Now, as then, a good architect will kill for between 120 and 150 acres of gently undulating land which has a spade's depth of light or sandy loam above a good subsoil. Add good natural drainage, an abundance of mature trees, with one or two streams and the odd natural lake, and you will be just about on the mark.

Unfortunately, one thing which has not remained the same is cost. Whereas Old Tom Morris would have knocked off a layout in less than a day and charged around £50, the same service from Jack Nicklaus would now cost a cool million dollars. And that's just for the design!

GREAT COURSES OF THE WORLD

Old Course, St Andrews

Golf has been played over the linksland of St Andrews for at least 500 years – probably for a couple of centuries more than that. It is the world's oldest surviving course.

In those early days of golf there was only a narrow, winding strip of open grass between rolling sand dunes and banks of gorse and heather. A succession of 11 holes were played northwards from the ancient cathedral and university city to the Eden estuary. Players then turned around and played back over the same stretch of land to exactly the same holes.

The 22-hole course was eventually condensed to 18 and the passage of time, and the enthusiastic hacking of thousands of golfers, gradually widened the fairways to allow those on the outward half to keep to the left, while homeward-bound golfers stayed closer to the North Sea shore, playing to different holes on the same greens on the way back.

Even today there is virtually no separation of outward and homeward fairways, except for the occasional cluster of hidden bunkers or outcrop of heather. Seven massive double greens bear witness to the origins of the course.

The course is now played in reverse order – the outward holes to the right – although 'the left-

Victory for Nick Faldo in the 1990 Open at St Andrews – the home of golf.

The backdrop of the R and A frames the Swilken Bridge, crossed by every player on their way up to the 18th.

hand course' is sometimes played in winter to give golfers a taste of times past.

Conditions have obviously changed a great deal over the centuries. The need to water and fertilise the course to preserve the precious turf from the onslaught of the world's golfers has softened its dry, fast-running nature to a large extent.

Yet the last major change was the removal of a bunker from the wide expanse of the 1st and 18th fairways in 1914, and the essential challenge of links golf as played five centuries ago remains intact.

Although there is room to drive safely to the left on most holes, the perfect line to attack championship pin positions is almost invariably close to the right edge. Many bunkers are hidden, some are large enough only 'for an angry man and his niblick', all require a skilful recovery shot.

Golfers reared on modern courses, where every problem is visible and where the ball stops quickly on soft greens, may find the Old Course infuriating on first acquaintance. But the ever-changing wind, the humps and hollows and the subtle borrows of large greens make every round at St Andrews a new test of patience and ability.

The prevailing south-west wind is across the line from the left at six of the outward holes and consequently from the opposite flank on the way home. An early morning whisper of wind can freshen in the afternoon, swing through 180 degrees and drop to a murmur by evening.

The 172-yard 11th hole has been played by Jack Nicklaus with an eight-iron and a three-iron in the same championship. The force of the wind helped shape the contours of the course and it continues to play a vital role in the hypnotic challenge of links golf.

Every champion in the history of the game has played these same fairways and the ultimate accolade is still to be crowned Open champion on the Old Course.

Muirfield

The Honourable Company of Edinburgh Golfers has continuous records going back to 1744, when they approached Edinburgh City Council for a silver club to be played for annually, establishing them as the oldest golf club in the world. Their members were also responsible for setting down the first written rules, and their course at Muirfield is regarded by many of the great players as the game's finest and fairest test of links golf.

The 13th green at Muirfield slopes sharply up from the front, and as the hole is often played downwind, club selection is vital. A six-foot deep bunker on the left of the green catches many shots.

Muirfield's 18th hole is one of the most challenging finishes in golf. A huge island bunker to the right of the green catches any mis-hit approach.

The club started in more humble surroundings, over the five-hole course at Leith, moving on to avoid public congestion first to Musselburgh and finally, in 1891, to their own private course at Muirfield. Some 20 years earlier the club had joined with Prestwick and St Andrews in taking responsibility for the Open Championship.

The year after their move along the southern shore of the Firth of Forth, it was the turn of the Honourable Company to host the first championship to be played over 72 holes instead of 36. Amateur Harold Hilton beat a field of 66 players with a score of 305, a total not bettered until 1905.

Since then Muirfield has been the scene of many epic Opens, from the American breakthrough in 1929 by Walter Hagen to the home victory by Nick Faldo in 1987. The list of champions – Henry Cotton, Gary Player, Jack Nicklaus, Lee Trevino and Tom Watson have all won at Muirfield – gives a clear indication of the quality of the course.

In many respects it is unlike the majority of links courses. Set above and well back from the shore line, with magnificent views across the broad waters of the Firth of Forth to the distant haze of Fife, the layout is extremely modern.

The opening nine holes complete a clockwise circle back to the clubhouse, with the second half running roughly in an anti-clockwise inner loop. Never more than three holes in succession face the same direction and there is a constant need to check the angles and strength of the wind. There is one blind tee-shot and the green at the uphill, short 13th is not visible – but the trouble on either side is.

On every other hole the problems are clearly in view, if not easily avoided. The rough at Muirfield grows rather more thickly than at most links courses and is subtly used to define and shape fairways. Bunkers are positioned and contoured in such a way that they tend to gather the ball into their depths and the combination of rough and sand puts a high premium on accurate driving.

Looking to defend his title in 1972, Lee Trevino was level with playing partner Tony Jacklin on the 17th tee. Jacklin hit the perfect tee-

The 18th green and unmistakeable clubhouse at Royal Birkdale.

shot out to the right past the bunkers and a second to the heart of the green. Trevino tried to cut the corner too closely and finished in a bunker. 'We've blown the championship right here,' he said to his caddy as they strode up the fairway. But he was wrong. After four dispirited shots he was over the green, hit a chip shot almost on the run – and holed it for a par five. Jacklin three-putted from nowhere and lost a championship that looked to be his for the taking.

Yet Muirfield seldom offers players the sort of bonus it gave Trevino. It is essentially a fair and honest course. There are few unkind bounces and good shots get the reward they deserve. But as strokes slip further and further away from perfection the punishment very properly fits the crime.

It is this element of 'getting what you hit' that makes Muirfield such a popular choice with the world's leading players in the Open. Jack Nicklaus recognised its merits as a young Walker Cup player and when he built his own golf course in Ohio he asked permission to name it Muirfield Village – an eloquent testimony to its eternal challenge.

Royal Birkdale

In a relatively short space of time Royal Birkdale has established itself as one of Britain's leading championship courses. It was first selected as an Open venue in 1940, but the world had more on its mind than golf in that year and when the great sporting events were re-scheduled after the war it took until 1954 before the club achieved Open status. Since then it has hosted the Open championship seven times, twice staged the Ryder Cup and been the scene of many leading amateur and professional events.

Set in a vast expanse of wild dune country on the Lancashire coast, Birkdale first felt the tread of golfing feet in 1889, when a group of local sportsmen agreed a £5-a-year lease on the land. The original course was re-shaped by JH Taylor and Fred Hawtree in the 1930s, but the club has never been content to sit back on past merits and many additional changes have been carried out since Peter Thomson won his and Birkdale's first Open in 1954.

The rolling sand dunes of Royal Birkdale – a
perfect example of a classic links course.

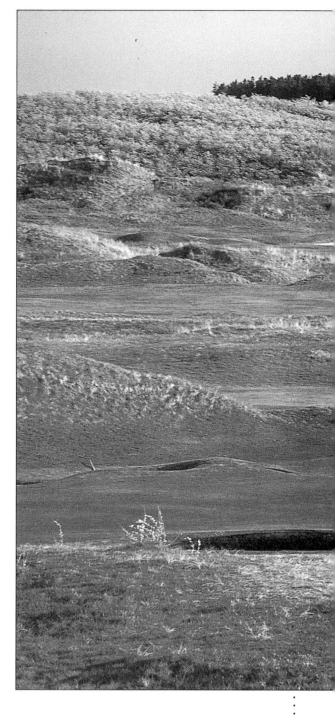

The short 17th hole was removed before the 1965 championship and replaced with a superb new par three at the 12th. Set in the giant dunes at the closest point the course reaches to the sea, it has been described by multiple Open champion Tom Watson as 'maybe the best short hole in British golf.'

This re-positioning of the short hole set up a gigantic finish to the course, with four of the final six holes measuring over 500 yards. Yet three of them are played down the prevailing south-west wind, and with the enormous power of today's professionals and the continuing improvement in equipment, they became easily reachable in two shots.

Rather than stretch the course even further, Birkdale decided to retain the essential playing characteristics of the holes by shortening two of them to just within the par-four limits, as well as tightening up the line of the tee shot and the approach to the green by slightly enlarging or re-shaping bunkers.

The effect has been dramatic, creating some of the best and most testing holes in championship golf and bringing the course to a much better-balanced conclusion.

Although often within sound of the sea, particularly when the prevailing wind pounds waves high on the shore line, the golfer who stays on or close to the fairways will catch only the odd, distant glint of water, for although the setting is traditional links terrain at its best, Birkdale's holes wind through distinct valleys in the shelter of the giant sand hills.

There are few of the rippling humps and hollows and difficult stances which are a feature of many seaside links. The fairways are essentially flat and greens are cut into the dunes, standing out as well-defined and clear targets. But not only are they protected by deep bunkers, the thick, clinging rough is allowed to grow within feet of the putting surfaces and the whole area abounds with ground-hugging willow scrub. Those who stray off-line at Birkdale pay a high price.

One man who made light work of the dreaded willow scrub was Arnold Palmer. A plaque on the right edge of the 16th fairway commemorates one of the great shots in golfing history. Fighting to cling on to a slender lead in the final round of the 1961 Open, Palmer's tee shot at what was then the 15th hole finished on a bank in heavy rough under a small bush. A mighty smash with a six-iron removed grass and bush in a cloud of flying debris and put the ball on the green 140 yards away against a strong wind. It was a shot which won him the title.

Peter Thomson returned to collect his fifth Open crown at Birkdale in 1965 and Tom Watson joined the elite band of five-time victors over the same course in 1983. Lee Trevino and Johnny Miller were winners here in the 1970s and Ian Baker-Finch added to the Australian tally of titles in 1991.

Tom O'Brien (right), head greenkeeper at Royal Birkdale.

Portmarnock

If true links courses are areas of wild, unspoiled duneland in close touch with the sea, then Portmarnock is doubly blessed. Laid out on a long thin finger of land which separates Dublin Bay from the Irish Sea, the course has water on three sides. And because of its remote situation and the fact that the course takes up the entire area at the point of the peninsula, no modern development has encroached to spoil the natural tranquility.

The setting has, in fact, changed very little since the day in 1893 when two local sportsmen rowed themselves across the estuary and discovered a potential golfing paradise inhabited by a small community of farming and fishing families.

No roads penetrated the peninsula at that time and when the course was opened the only access for golfers at high tide was by means of a ferry from Sutton, although a horse-drawn carriage could make the dash across the sands with the tide at its lowest ebb. The small wooden shack which served as the first clubhouse has long since been replaced by a large and elegant white-walled, red-tiled haven, and roads have replaced rowing boats as a means of getting to the course.

The course, too, has developed from the original nine holes which Scottish professional Mungo Park helped the founders of the club to design. Within four years a full 18 holes were in operation, and although it was not until the 1970s that Fred Hawtree was asked to lay out a further nine holes, there is plenty of room for another course amid the isolation of the dunes.

In addition to being a regular host to the Irish Open, Portmarnock has also staged the Dunlop Masters and was selected in 1949 as the only venue outside the United Kingdom ever to hold the British Amateur Championship.

International honours came in 1960 when Portmarnock was chosen as the venue for the Canada Cup, now the World Cup. That event was the first time the legendary Arnold Palmer had played east of the Atlantic and he immediately

The 15th at Portmarnock – arguably the best course in Ireland.

showed an instinctive ability for links golf, partnering Sam Snead to an eight-shot victory. Players on the European tour have voted Portmarnock the best tournament venue.

Further recognition of the qualities of the course came in 1991 when Great Britain and Ireland's finest amateurs failed to add to their previous successes over America in the Walker Cup – the first time the event had been held in Ireland.

Because the course is laid out across, rather than along, the peninsula, the holes are constantly changing direction. Each nine describes an approximate anti-clockwise double loop back to the clubhouse. In practical terms this means that whatever the strength and direction of the wind there is no way to escape its effect on the ball from all angles, for at no point on the course do more than two consecutive holes run in the same direction.

The sand dunes are never large enough to give more than token protection from the elements, although many fairways curve through natural shallow valleys. This is traditional links golf at its best – crisp turf, deep bunkers set within the contours of the ground rather than being artificially raised, and fast greens with subtle rather than massive borrows.

In the light breezes of summer there can be no finer place to enjoy the game. And when the wind whips a salt-water spray over the fairways, it can be one of golf's most severe tests.

Plateau greens are the feature of many Irish links courses; here at the 15th the wind affects every shot.

The impressive Portmarnock clubhouse which looks out across the Irish Sea.

Pinehurst

Pinehurst is the St Andrews of American golf – a small, traditional community dominated by its seven golf courses. And at the heart of this golfing paradise lies the world-famous Number 2 course, designed and perfected by Donald Ross, a Scot who learned his trade under Old Tom Morris in St Andrews.

The Pinehurst story started with the successful Boston pharmacist James W. Tufts. In order to escape the harsh New England winters, he was searching for a holiday home further south in 1897 when he was made an offer he felt unable to refuse. For one dollar an acre he could have 5000 acres of land from which the pine trees had been cut. Inspired by the rapid growth of golf in the New York and New England area, he set out to create a winter playground for refugees from the cold.

Pinehurst Country Club's Number 1 course was a fairly rough and ready affair when Harry

Vardon was invited to play it in 1900, but his visit triggered off a great deal of local interest and led to the appointment of a young Scottish professional called Donald Ross.

Born and brought up in Dornoch in Scotland's far north east, he had served an apprenticeship under Old Tom Morris before taking over the job of professional and greenkeeper at his home course. In December of 1900 he arrived in Pinehurst to take up a similar position.

Within a year he had started work on the Number 2 course, but his painstaking efforts were slow in coming to fruition and it was not until 1907 that the second 18-hole course came into play.

It was immediately recognised as an outstanding course, but Ross was far from satisfied and he continued to make adjustments and improvements over the years. Many of the changes which Ross felt compelled to make were brought about by the vast improvements in golfing equipment which allowed players to hit the ball further.

Pinehurst – the clubhouse contains not the 19th hole but the 91st!

An impressive hotel provides golfing guests with all the luxury they can handle.

Right: *The 4th on course No. 2 – the Golf Hall of Fame in the background contains the very best of golfing memorabilia as well as honouring the sport's great heroes.*

The 6th at Pinehurst No. 2, the best course on the complex.

Just how good a job Ross did in those early years of the century can be seen by the fact that Pinehurst Number 2 has retained its position as one of the great courses of the world and has refused to be overwhelmed by the modern power-hitters.

The trees that had been cut back so drastically when Tufts was able to buy the land have regenerated to such an extent that every hole is played between pines in a little private oasis of golfing tranquility. The course now measures just

over 7000 yards from the championship tees, but its challenge lies in its subtlety and its demands on accuracy rather than mere yards.

Ross learned his golf at Dornoch, where many greens are slightly raised and protected by slopes and hollows as well as bunkers. This became part of his strategy at Pinehurst, where the optimum angle for approach shots to relatively small greens can often only be achieved with absolute precision from the tee.

All this was achieved by using the natural contours of the ground, not with any massive programme of earth-moving, and the overall result is the most marvellous combination of fine, crisp turf – quick-draining on its sandy base – gentle contouring and clever bunkering, in a tree-lined setting.

This is fine, old, subtle golf, rich in character and variety, endlessly challenging and more than a match for today's great players.

Augusta National

Bobby Jones looked for perfection in everything he did. As a lawyer he built up a thriving and successful practice. As a golfer he took the world by storm, climaxing an amazing career by winning the Open and Amateur Championships of Britain and America in one glorious season. As a golf course designer he left Augusta National by which to be judged.

He was only 28 when he won all four major titles in one year – an accomplishment that later

became known as the Grand Slam – and he had no wish to become a professional. He retired from competitive golf but harboured a dream to create a fine new course for exclusive use by a small number of friends.

At precisely that moment the perfect piece of land came on the market: 365 acres of rolling terrain which had been a fruit, flower and shrub nursery. Jones, together with New York lawyer Clifford Roberts, snapped up the property and called on Dr Alister Mackenzie to help with the design. The Scots medical man had shown a rare talent for golf course creation in Britain and had

Jones hit thousands of experimental shots from suggested tee positions and redefined green sites by hitting approach shots from a wide variety of angles. The course was completed by 1933 but not opened for play until the following year, shortly after Mackenzie died.

To mark the birth of the new course Jones invited many friends from the ranks of amateur and professional golf to take part in a tournament. He was essentially a modest and unpretentious man and resisted many suggestions for grandiose titles for the event, calling it simply the Augusta National Invitation. But such was the response from all the great players in the game that the press were calling it the Masters before the four rounds were completed. Every year since it has become the opening event of the modern Grand Slam.

Jones was constantly making small changes to the course, a process which continues today in

Left: *The water at Augusta has claimed many a victim. Here at the par five 15th only the longest hitters will carry the 500 yards to the green in two.*

Below: *By now the heat is really on – the 18th tee at Augusta. Many would-be champions have known they need a par here.*

emigrated to America in order to pursue his new career.

Jones had fallen under the spell of links golf while winning his titles in Scotland and although he had no intention of trying to copy specific links holes on his undulating inland site, he was determined to recreate something of the feel of the traditional game at Augusta.

So the finest player in the world and one of the leading design experts got together to create a modern course with a traditional feel over one of the most beautiful stretches of land in the Southern states. During the period of the design,

Getting a ticket for the Masters can take a lifetime – some of the fortunate few enjoy the flower-bordered walkways between holes.

The Pacific mist looms eerily over the bay as the backdrop to the par three 7th at Pebble Beach – a hole which demands a tee-shot of unerring accuracy.

pursuit of ever-elusive perfection. After only one year he switched the outward and homeward nines and it is surprising today to think that he ever contemplated playing the course the other way round, for the closing nine is by far the more demanding, featuring water at five holes, where there is none on the outward half.

Jones designed the course primarily for friends who might not be world beaters, but he also wanted it to be a fitting challenge for the great players. Fairways are generously and invitingly wide and bunkers are sparingly used – seven holes have no fairway bunkering at all. There is very little rough and the greens are large but extremely fast.

The average player who scores in the mid-eighties will probably have no trouble in hitting most greens in regulation, but scoring at Augusta is all about planning each hole backwards from the pin position. So severe are the green contours that approach shots must be hit below the hole. In order to achieve this, tee shots must be accurate to within a few yards. Nobody scores well at the Masters without a careful plan and the ability to carry it out.

Pebble Beach

When the United States Golf Association relented in the face of continuing pressure and played the 1929 Amateur Championship at Pebble Beach, it was the first national championship to be staged west of the Mississippi. The magnificent and beautiful Monterey Peninsula, sharply jutting into the Pacific from the Californian coast, had finally arrived on the golfing map.

Until then it was considered too remote, being some 120 miles south of San Francisco, for big-time golf, although it had been the scene of more than one Californian state event. Now the golfing world beats a path to Pebble's first tee and there are not enough daylight hours to accommodate those who want to play one of the world's truly great and scenic courses.

The whole peninsula has become a golfing playground, with superb courses such as Cypress Point and Spyglass Hill nestling one against the other around the rocky clifftops.

Unusually for an American course, Pebble Beach does not have two convenient loops of nine

For sheer spectacle it would be hard to find a more beautiful golf hole in the world than the 17th at Pebble Beach.

holes meeting back at the clubhouse, but spreads itself out along the shore and turns homeward from the distant 10th green. But unlike the old Scottish links courses, where fairways are often at sea level and views are blocked out by large sand dunes, the holes at Pebble Beach are laid out along the low cliffs, some 50 or 60 feet above the Pacific surf. Many of the world's great golfers, including Arnold Palmer and Jack Nicklaus, have played shots from the rocks and the beach back up to greens perched perilously close to the cliff edge.

Nicklaus won the third Amateur Championship to be played here in 1961 by a crushing 8 and 6 margin over Dudley Wysong and came back 11 years later to take the first Open Championship played on the course.

In typically difficult Californian coastal weather, Nicklaus mastered the strong winds for a final round of 74 and a two-over-par total of 290. He sealed victory with a controlled one-iron which hit the stick at the par-three 17th.

At the same hole 10 years later, Nicklaus was fighting for his fifth US Open title and was tied with Tom Watson, who was chasing his first Open win. Nicklaus hit the green but Watson was in thick grass just off the fringe. Yet in an inspired spell, Watson holed that recovery shot and birdied the final hole as well to defeat Nicklaus by two shots.

After a quiet inland start, the third hole heads towards the sea and the fourth is the first of the clifftop holes. The par-five sixth is played out onto a promontory, with the sea again cutting in on the right. The seventh is probably the shortest championship hole in America – only 120 yards downhill to a green only eight paces wide and surrounded by sand and sea. On a still day it can be an easy wedge shot. With the wind off the Pacific it can be a full three-iron.

Then follow the three toughest holes on the course – three par-fours of well over 400 yards, each played along the clifftop with the sea to the right and the greens cut uncomfortably close to the rocks. The course then turns inland through the edge of the Del Monte Forest before coming dramatically back to the rugged coastline for the two final holes.

The views over Stillwater Cove and Monterey Bay are spectacular and basking seals often catch the eye on the rocks below. It is difficult not to let the concentration slip and watch the ball join them.

Lanny Wadkins managed it successfully when he won the PGA Championship here in 1977 and competitors in the 1992 Open were faced with the same task when the title was contested for the third time over this most spectacular course.

Valderrama

Robert Trent Jones, America's high-profile, prolific course designer, first made his entry into Europe with 36 holes at Sotogrande on the Costa del Sol in Spain in 1965.

The American influence was unmistakable. Vast teeing areas, massive greens, enormous bunkers and lots of water – all the Trent Jones hallmarks were very evident. And these courses became role models for the other developments which mushroomed along Spain's southern coast.

The quality of the turf in the early days was a revelation for golf course builders in Europe. Bermuda grass was imported and developed in nurseries on the site for use on the fairways and after a few early experiments Pencross bent was sown on the greens. This was the same seed which had proved so successful on many prestigious American courses such as Augusta National and was particularly suited to the climate of southern Spain.

The Los Aves course, looking down on the village of Sotogrande, was chosen by Severiano Ballesteros for his final two weeks of practice before setting off to America for the 1983 Masters. He felt it had many of the characteristics of the Augusta course, with its severe demands on accuracy off the tee and into the greens, and the putting surfaces were some of the quickest in Europe.

After he had won his second Masters title a few days later he met Trent Jones in the Augusta National clubhouse and gave much of the credit for his success to the practice he had recently completed on the American's Spanish course. That course has since been remodelled and

renamed. In 1985 it was bought by wealthy Jaime Ortiz-Patino and a small group of his golfing friends.

Trent Jones was invited to look again at his original design and make any improvements he felt necessary. He had always believed the course was one of his finest achievements and relished the idea of 'polishing the diamond'. With small and sometimes seemingly insignificant changes he has tightened the driving line a fraction on some holes, put greater demands on the approach shots at others, and enhanced the contours at some points and made them more subtle elsewhere.

Left: *Classic Andalucian architecture inside the clubhouse at Valderrama. Outside are rows of orange trees.*

In its new guise and under the new name of Valderrama, the course was chosen as the setting for the Volvo Masters, the concluding event of the season. In a short space of time it has established itself as a very fitting scene for the climax to the European tour and has won praise and a great deal of respect from the leading professionals.

Rising and falling dramatically through a profusion of cork trees, the course does not rely on excessive length to get the best from players as some of Trent Jones' other creations have done. Here the challenge is more subtle, demanding extreme accuracy from the tee in order to hit the ball into the correct part of the green to take advantage of the variety of pin positions.

From the championship tees the professionals find it one of the toughest tests in Europe, particularly the back nine and especially the four closing holes. It is a course which needs to be outsmarted, not bullied into submission. It requires thought and careful club selection by pros and amateurs alike.

Royal Melbourne

Immigrants from St Andrews were among the founder members of the Royal Melbourne Golf Club in 1891. So well had their fellow members been indoctrinated with traditional ideas from the home of golf that when they were seeking to move their course for the third time in 1924 they snapped up the chance of a large area of sand dunes covered in heather, bracken and small trees.

They also invited Alister Mackenzie, the Scots doctor who gave up medicine in favour of golf course design and later worked with Bobby Jones to create Augusta National, to lay out their new course.

Mackenzie was in his element and he was joined by that year's Australian Open champion Alex Russell in building a course with a truly Scottish flavour in a foreign land. After the success of the West course, Russell worked alone

An oasis of green set against the stark, awe-inspiring mountains of the Sierra Bermeja – the 15th at Valderrama.

The 6th hole (composite) at Royal Melbourne is a terror! A sharp dog-leg is protected by four horrible bunkers 230 yards off the tee, pushing the drive left. That leaves a 200-yard carry to a closely guarded green.

The 11th (composite – 17th West) is another dog-leg with bunkers protecting the turn. Eucalyptus trees line the fairway too, closing it down even more. The green has only one bunker – but it's 50 yards long!

to produce the equally testing and attractive East course.

When the club was selected to host the 1959 Canada Cup (later World Cup) a composite course was used for the first time. This was considered necessary to avoid the roads which cross both courses. The combined layout consisted of 12 holes from the original and six from the East, together forming a course which is regarded by leading players as one of the world's finest.

A feature of the Melbourne course is the way the natural undergrowth is allowed to tumble over the fairway edges and creep right up to, and even into, bunkers. There are many islands of shrub and long rough surrounded by sand. It gives a very natural appearance, in sharp contrast to the more precise and formal presentation of many modern courses where it sometimes appears that no blade of grass should be out of place.

The man largely responsible for the special Melbourne look was the former head greenkeeper Claude Crockford. He was a man of great vision and influence and he nurtured the designs of Mackenzie and Russell into a comprehensive 36-hole complex.

When members and professionals began to doubt the wisdom of Mackenzie's short seventh hole, where the green was above the level of the tee and therefore invisible to the golfer, Crockford undertook its redesign. He whittled away at the slopes with horse-drawn scoops and created a new and beautifully contoured green at a lower level. He protected it with deep bunkers and a front slope covered with long grass and shrub.

Crockford was also the man responsible for the Melbourne greens being regarded as some of the best in the world. In order to prevent root disease in the grasses, he would lift the turf, scrape away the topsoil and the lower levels of the grass roots and replace it with fresh soil. Each green was treated in this way on a 15 to 18 year cycle, a painstaking process which has had long-lasting results.

Apart from the firm, supremely true greens and the overall condition of the course, the lure of Royal Melbourne lies in its fine variety of holes, particularly the par fours where the challenge is just as intriguing at the 305-yard 8th as it is over the 470-yard 14th. The 8th green has been driven,

but in competitive play few would attempt to carry across the valley and truly cavernous bunker and trees. Yet to play safe leaves a pitch to a small, tightly trapped green.

The tee shot at the 14th must carry enormous bunkers which fill the skyline before the fairway drops downhill. Only the very best drive will set up a second shot back up to the green which is angled off to the right behind a line of three bunkers.

The fact that Royal Melbourne is the only course to be chosen three times for the World Cup speaks volumes for its pre-eminence in the southern hemisphere.

Chantilly

Although France can claim the first golf course in mainland Europe, built at Pau in the Pyrenees for the Duke of Hamilton in 1856, there were few further golfing developments in the country before Chantilly was created in 1908.

Set in the edge of the forest just 25 miles north of Paris, the original 18 holes were put under the close scrutiny of Tom Simpson in 1920. He carried out a great deal of redesign work, comprehensively lengthening and upgrading the holes in line with more traditionally accepted standards. By moving tee positions to change the angles of play and making more imaginative use of the existing trees, he was able to eliminate large numbers of rather bland bunkers which had been added in unsuccessful attempts to give the course more bite.

Simpson was also commissioned to design a new 18-hole course and until the Second World War Chantilly was one of the few clubs in Europe or Britain to have the use of two full courses. But parts of his new layout did not survive the conflict and rather than rebuild, the second course was reduced to nine holes.

Within five years of its inauguration Chantilly was playing host to the French Open Championship, won by Scotsman George Duncan. Henry Cotton captured the title here in 1947 and the popular Argentinian Roberto de Vicenzo showed his immense liking for the course by winning the

Previous page: *The 6th hole at Chantilly – a devilishly difficult 215-yard par three to a downhill green that slopes front to back.*

Above: *Approaching the 18th green – in the background is the clubhouse, a fine example of Norman architecture.*

French crown there both in 1950 and again in 1964. When the championship returned 10 years later it was the turn of giant Englishman Peter Oosterhuis, and then there was a long gap until Chantilly came back into the limelight, hosting three French Opens in a row from 1988. The first two were won by Nick Faldo and the third by Philip Walton of Ireland after a play-off with Bernhard Langer.

Although Chantilly is built in a forest setting, there are very few holes where the trees crowd in on the line of play. There is an overall impression of space, with generous fairways and comfortable areas of light rough for an errant shot to cover before getting into the woods.

One place where there is little room for error is at the fourth where the view from the tee is down a claustrophobic avenue of trees. Those not totally confident of staying on the straight and narrow might be well advised to hit something less than the driver here, particularly as the hole is well under 400 yards. But it is not wise to overdo the cautious play because the green is very tightly bunkered at the front. It is a hole that requires fine judgement.

From the back tees the par fives are awesome. There are only three of them, but any imbalance in length is compensated by the fact that three of the short holes are more than 200 yards. Unfortunately two of the long holes come at the eighth and ninth, with the final par five being saved to the very end of the round. This is a true monster, just a handful of paces short of 600 yards, but the tee shot is downhill before the ground rises again towards the green.

Playing downwind in 1974 Peter Oosterhuis reached the green with a one-iron from the tee and a three-wood second shot for a closing birdie. When Roberto de Vicenzo won the French Open in 1964 he was clumsy enough to be through the green in two shots, but chipped back safely for a four.

Climbing and dipping through gently undulating woodland and wonderful open vistas, the course changes direction constantly and almost every green is temptingly set against a backdrop of trees. Driving is an important part of the game at Chantilly and accuracy is often the wiser choise than length. It is a course on which a golfer's full range of second shots will be well tested.

Hirono

Over the past 20 years Japan has experienced a golfing explosion without equal anywhere in the world. In a country where only 17 per cent of the mountainous land mass is suitable for cultivation, the pressure on space for developing golf courses is enormous.

As a consequence massive feats of earth-moving have been carried out so that the Japanese can play a sport which has become synonymous with wealth and success. Whole mountain-sides have been blasted into valleys to create golfing space. Many courses have escalators between holes to carry golfers back up steep hillsides to the next tee.

The American influence is strong – lakes and massive areas of sand are key features – and the majority of Japanese courses could be transplanted in Florida without a single golfer noticing the difference. Yet despite this rash of ultra-modernism, the country's more knowledge-able golfers keep returning to, and learning from, the Hirono course near the major port of Kobe.

Designed by Englishman Charles Alison in 1930, it is a timeless example of subtle, traditional golfing qualities; a little piece of Japan that will be forever Sunningdale. Alison was the type of architect who liked to use the natural contours of the ground as much as possible and he was lucky in the choice of site, a generous acreage which needed none of the earth-moving programmes required by most modern courses. Streams ran through the undulating area of pine trees into small lakes.

An accomplished artist, Alison could visualise a demanding and difficult test of golf which made the most of the terrain and he was also able to sketch out in great detail exactly how he wished every hole to look. Many of his working diagrams and completed drawings are still in the club's possession.

Three of the short holes are across water, but with generous room for the handicap golfer. Yet Alison's genius is probably best appreciated at the par-three seventh where he has sited the green against a backdrop of trees on the far side of two large depressions. He has cut bunkers into the natural slopes and allowed the undergrowth to tumble into the hollows. Out of nothing he has created a hole which looks as though it was fashioned by nature.

Perhaps the strongest hole on the course is the par-five 12th, where the club player has a small, safe target area of fairway between the lake and a stream which feeds into it, but where the professionals are expected to carry both.

From the championship tees there are many long carries over rough to well-bunkered fairways, but the handicap golfer is always given a fair crack of the whip. Even the holes which bring the lakes into play never demand too much of the golfer who plays for fun.

'A little piece of Japan that is forever Sunningdale.'

The course that Jack built – Muirfield Village, Ohio.

THE GREENKEEPERS

DURING an average week a golf course is played by anything up to 1500 golfers. Each of them will hit between 80 and perhaps 95 shots, many of them taking divots – not all of which will be replaced.

Each green – a fairly small area – will have 1500 golf balls landing on it, often leaving a pitch mark. Then the same number of pairs of feet will walk round it, leaving 30000 spike marks, particularly near the hole.

Every golfer wants the greens flat and true, without humps or bumps to knock the putt off line; the rough should not be too long, the fairways not too wet, the bunkers well raked and filled with soft sand which will allow even the worst hacker to splash the ball out comfortably.

The average fairway is around 2 acres, so apart from the greens which need extra care, the greenkeeping staff have over 36 acres of land to keep in tip-top condition, plus a considerable further amount to look after.

During a good summer in northern Europe, with average rainfall and good sunshine for grass growth, that is not too much of a problem if well planned. But in the dark days of winter when growth is non-existent and greens and fairways are liable to receive persistent, heavy rain, the outlook, like the sky, is pretty bleak.

In the United States, where heavy summer rainfall is not so common, fairways have to receive large amounts of water from irrigation systems and the greens staff can almost dictate whether a fairway will be hard and bouncy, like a traditional British seaside links course, or lush and holding, which most American golfers prefer.

Whatever the situation, the people who go about their job of cutting the grass, tending the greens and generally keeping the golf course in top condition are an unsung part of golf's success story. Yet without them the courses just would not be fit to play.

Going back to the last century, many of the professionals of the day were also greenkeepers – Old Tom Morris moved to Prestwick to tend the greens, being given a wheelbarrow by the club to help him. The equipment these days has changed considerably!

Irrigation systems have also transformed golf courses, allowing them to be kept green nearly all year round, in spite of droughts, in Britain at least, at the end of the 1980s.

St Pierre, near Chepstow in South Wales, has been host for several years to a major European Tour event, the Epson Grand Prix. Getting the course into condition for Europe's top professionals is an extra strain on the greenkeeping staff, led by Course Manager David Jones.

Professionals like to have the greens shorter – and thus faster – than the average club player. Normally the greens are cut to a height of 3/16ths of an inch, which allows them to continue growing. For professional tournaments they are cut to just

The moment every greenkeeper dreads. Violent thunderstorms on the third day of the 1989 US Open flood this bunker at Oak Hill.

Pin positions are moved daily to provide even wear on the greens.

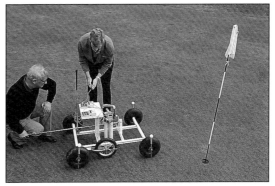

Not a new racing car! This odd-looking machine in fact measures the gradients on a green to within a few millimetres.

1/8th of an inch, which really is too low to permit continued growth. Keeping the grass that low hinders growth, so although the players late in the day will see little difference from those out early, a long period of cutting to that height would kill the grass.

Professionals these days, playing for huge stakes where one missed putt can mean a loss of several thousand pounds, like to take all the chance out of their game, so the greens have to be as perfect as possible, with no 'crowning' around

In extreme cases greenkeepers will even employ fan-heaters to dry a green out.

the hole. The approach areas, and those places where a missed approach might land, are also very carefully tended so that there are, in essence, no bad bounces in a pro golf tournament. Whether this is fair on the average club golfer, who has to contend with many such poor bounces and difficult lies, is a perennial question, but professional golfers, with all their extra shot-making skills, do have an 'easier' course to play.

Of course, spike marks on the green each day will mean an inevitable deterioration for the late players – ironically, on the last two days anyway, the tournament leaders.

Planning for the tournament begins many months in advance but it is in the last three months that changes in the golf course are clearly discernible. The rough is allowed to grow so that it can be cut back to a standard height just before the tournament begins. The fairways are also trimmed to give an area of semi-rough just six feet wide, following the contours of the fairway.

The fairways themselves are re-shaped slightly, giving a wider landing area at about 240 yards off the tee, and all fairways are tended to ensure that no divot marks remain. Normally play on the course itself is restricted in the week or two preceding the tournament proper, which helps the grass to strengthen.

This is the case on the greens, too, where in the five or six weeks before the tournament, the grass is cut vertically to help get it standing up straight. The greens are also top-dressed, building up the surface around the blades of grass rather than actually increasing the grass itself.

Grass grows in little air bubbles around the

root rather than in compacted earth, so aerating is also necessary to increase growth. All that good work is, sadly, undone once the tournament begins, the grass being cut back to give a better surface.

The greens normally need watering too, unless heavy rain falls for several weeks. The sprinklers (normally four) on each green are individually controlled to give an even spread of water, yet even here there is some overlap, leading to certain areas being slightly wetter than they should. Professionals like the fronts of greens to

be watered, to hold approach shots better. For David Jones it is an interference with his year-long aim of growing grass, but a pleasure to see his course shown to millions on television!

Each green varies in the amount of water it needs per day and that depends on rainfall. Each sprinkler normally dispenses 15 gallons per minute; the average green needs between six and nine minutes' irrigation a day without natural rainfall.

The fairways need watering too, with about two gallons per square yard per day being the

Above: *Tiny particles of loose sand and soil are blown away with this machine.*

Left: *Modern machinery can evenly cut a green to a height of 1/8th of an inch.*

Below: *Looking as if he's about to fly away on this broomstick a greenkeeper takes a brief break.*

norm, again without normal rainfall. Each fairway receives around 20 000 gallons per week. In the week before the tournament, the fairways are treated with a liquid mixture of seaweed and sulphate of iron, strengthening the grass and giving it that extra lush look we always see on television.

During the tournament itself, the grass is cut on the greens each morning, and of course the pin positions are changed daily. Although the greens staff cut the holes, the pin positions are chosen by the tournament director, though there

In the United States lower rainfall makes the watering of fairways a necessity. It also makes 'target golf' the game to play, the ball stopping quickly on landing.

To make the holes more visible, particularly for television, the inside of the cups are painted white.

The early-morning silence is broken only by birdsong and the sound of a motor mower as another day of golf begins.

may be occasions when the course manager might suggest alternative sitings, particularly if the weather forecast predicts rain. Most greens have an area where water might collect more and these are best avoided for pin positions. There are also, under some greens, hard, rocky areas which are difficult to cut through to make the hole.

One problem not generally recognised is that where a golf location such as St Pierre has two courses, the one not being used for the tournament still needs maintaining every day just the same. Work on the championship course needs to be concentrated in the early morning prior to play commencing and again in the evening after play has finished.

With many matches going on into the early evening as golfers take longer and longer over their rounds, that can leave precious little time in which to ensure that all the divots are replaced, bunkers raked, greens and fairways cut and watered and the spectator walkways and other areas in good condition.

By the time the greens staff have finished their day's work it is, quite often, almost time to get up again ready for first light and more work.

At St Pierre there are just 10 staff to help maintain the championship course in top condition and to ensure that the Mathern course is also kept in such a condition that it can easily be used the day after the main tournament finishes – the members do not like their courses out of action for too long, after all!

Becoming a greenkeeper these days involves a lot of hard work and study. College courses leading to recognised qualifications are attended, as well as the essential of practical work experience out on the course. Golf course maintenance differs considerably from other sports ground upkeep; like football or cricket pitches for example, both of which are only used intermittently.

As David Jones from St Pierre explains, his golf courses are used every day of the year except one, and the wear and tear is all concentrated in one area – despite club golfers' attempts to use the rough, the trees and the lake!

So perhaps understanding a little of what the greenkeeper's job entails might just persuade every golfer to replace every divot and repair every pitch-mark – but that's probably as likely as having every golfer go round in level par!

PART FOUR:
TOURNAMENTS

BEHIND THE SCENES

*F*OR the players and the fans, a tournament on the PGA European Tour lasts four days; but for the people responsible for staging the event it is almost a year-long project. No sooner has one tournament finished, amidst the presentation of large cheques and even larger bottles of champagne, than the planning meetings are arranged to discuss the following year.

The number and size of tournaments on the £16 million PGA European Tour has increased enormously since 1980 when total prize money was just £1.7 million. In those days there were 22 scheduled tournaments with an average of less than £60 000 in prize money – a dramatic contrast with 1991 when there were 42 tournaments and Tour-approved events, each worth an average of around £400 000. The season in Europe now runs from February to mid–November and outside that period the Tour is also involved with other events in Australia, the Far East and the Americas.

The figures reflect the tremendous growth of interest in golf among both commercial organisations, who value its potential as a promotional vehicle, and among ordinary fans whose enthusiasm was rekindled by the stirring achievements of Ballesteros, Langer, Lyle and others in the late 1970s and early 1980s. The success of the reborn European Ryder Cup team has played an enormous role in widening golf's appeal and starting a golfing boom unprecedented in the UK and Europe.

As the whole golf 'business' has expanded, its organisation and administration has by necessity become highly professional and sophisticated. Sponsors back tournaments with long-term commitments and millions of pounds because they believe there is commercial gain to be made in doing so and, quite reasonably, they expect their investment to be managed to provide the maximum return.

Their tournament, that one week in a year, has to be one of their main promotional vehicles. It must be made to sell the correct image for the sponsoring company and its products. Sponsorships have therefore to meet specific commercial objectives and if they do not, it is the wise sponsor

The old manor house (now the hotel) at St Pierre, Chepstow, is partly hidden behind the new leisure centre. Directly behind the flag on the 18th is the old church, dating back many hundreds of years.

who will withdraw and spend his promotional budget in other ways.

These facts of business life are well appreciated by everyone involved in running a tournament – the host club, the promoters, the PGA European Tour itself and the media. In particular, the Tour appreciate that without sponsors their spectacular growth would not have been possible and that many of their very prosperous players might have been locked into a life of selling tee pegs and correcting the captain's shank.

Thus there is the need for a planning cycle that leaves no detail, no area for improvement, no nicety undiscussed in the quest for making next year's tournament even better than the previous one.

The 1991 Epson Grand Prix of Europe, played at St Pierre, Chepstow in late September, was blessed by beautiful weather and a superb performance by José Maria Olazabal who won by nine shots.

The tournament, which regrettably turned out to be Epson's swansong, was a huge success but only because it had been in the planning stages since the previous December.

It was then that tournament director Michael Stewart of the PGA European Tour had his first meetings with the St Pierre authorities to discuss course preparation and any alterations which might be under consideration. At around the same time, BBC Television would reconnoitre the parkland course to find the most effective camera positions and to determine how best to cover St

Food, glorious food! Just a small selection of the day's provisions at a major golf tournament.

Pierre's picturesque new 17th green which would be played for the first time during the tournament.

Also involved in these early site meetings would be the sponsor's own tournament director from BD Sport Promotions, whose job it would be to see that every physical aspect of organisation was planned and placed correctly, arrived on time, functioned properly and operated within budget. Eventually, he would take up residence at St Pierre a month before the tournament and not leave until the last grandstand, stake and length of rope had been removed, up to 10 days after it had finished.

As a senior tournament director with the PGA European Tour, Michael Stewart was responsible for running 12 events in 1991. His is a demanding schedule involving much travel and long days, and requiring stamina, patience and the capacity to think clearly on the move.

'All that pre-planning is intended to eradicate or at least minimise the problems that might crop up during tournament week. It is in the interests of everyone for the event to run smoothly and by working closely with the host club, the sponsors

An early start is made to the greens, well before play commences.

and their promoters on the preparation, we can establish a team which slots together well,' he says.

Setting up the course correctly is a good example. 'If we do our planning correctly, we should avoid players having to call for endless rulings which just slows play down and frustrates everyone. Similarly, it is important that spectator walkways are thoughtfully sited – good for watchers but not distracting for players – and that stewards understand what they are required to do and how best to manage the movement of people.'

The Tour's agronomists may also be involved in the preparation and conditioning of the course in the six months leading up to the tournament. Their job is to work alongside the course manager or head greenkeeper to help them achieve the level of preparation required for a major event. The Tour will also provide consultant greenkeepers to support the club's own staff and work on the course for a short time prior to and during a tournament. This effective partnership between the club and the Tour not only benefits the tournament but also the home members, who gain the long-term advantage of the time, money and expertise which is put into their course.

When Michael Stewart and his team of two tournament administrators and two scorers/ secretaries arrived on the Sunday before the tournament, their temporary office was already in situ. From here they would run the playing side of the event in addition to acting as a branch office of Tour HQ at Wentworth.

Next door, in another mobile office, was the Epson tournament office, the nerve centre through which every aspect of the Grand Prix's organisation would be channelled. Through a network of radio links, the office would remain in constant touch with security, catering, electricians, plumbers, stewards, the police, on-course doctors, hotel management and the Press centre to ensure that any problems were quickly identified and corrected.

A prominent feature at every golf tournament is the tented village where companies can entertain clients in cosseted luxury and where spectators can find all the amenities required to make their day at the golf comfortable and enjoyable.

Organisation of the village is yet another job for the sponsor's promotional team and it includes selling hospitality pavilions, negotiating franchises

Modern communications keep events running smoothly. Pictured is Andy McFee of the PGA European Tour.

with businesses wishing to take space in the village and its exhibition area, and ensuring that the village is attractively and safely laid out.

The objective is to give visitors a good choice of catering – from silver service to hot snacks – and a comfortable environment in which to take a break from walking round the course. They can browse in the golf exhibition, peruse the giant scoreboard or even cash a cheque at the bank if they spot a new set of clubs that takes their fancy.

Providing food and drink in the private marquees and public restaurants at the Epson Grand Prix was the responsibility of event manager Ian Goodwin and his team from Payne and Gunter, one of the leaders in supplying hospitality at major sporting events. Planning is also the secret of their success and is very necessary if up to 500 full meals are to be served, beautifully prepared and piping hot during the course of a single day.

'This is a fairly low number compared with the Open where we often serve 3500 meals a day and then use the pavilions for dinners at night, but it still demands a lot of organisation,' says Ian whose working day is typically 6.30 am to 8 pm.

At St Pierre his company used 80 catering staff in addition to having eight of their own chefs on site. Earlier visits had helped determine the best place for the kitchens in relation to water and power supplies. Ovens and refrigerators are run off Calor Gas while the company also have a 40ft-long freezer trailer and a fridge-freezer unit on site to keep foods in perfect condition.

'We do contract some local companies to supply us with produce but most of the major items come from the large London markets. We pride ourselves on providing imaginative and high quality menus and it is vital therefore that the ingredients are of the best,' said Ian.

Payne and Gunter have a menu review meeting in January at which new ideas are discussed. 'We like to offer a wide and interesting choice but everything has to be a practical proposition in relation to the number of meals we have to serve and the facilities that are available,' Ian explained.

Presentation and service are also important elements in ensuring that guests have a memorable day and for this reason Payne and Gunter will often bring in regular and proven staff from considerable distances and accommodate them locally if necessary.

If the spectators and corporate guests are at a tournament for pure enjoyment, the members of the media are there on business and it is the job of the Press Officer and his staff to provide them with everything they need to report the event to the great golfing public.

The Epson Press Centre was designed to accommodate up to 150 journalists and its facilities included fax machines, telephones, photo-copiers, all-day refreshments and a back-up secretarial service.

The Press Centre at any tournament is one of the busiest places as deadlines for radio and newspapers come and go in unrelenting fashion. After a good round, a player may be required to undergo trial by interview in the Press Centre so that the media can report his innermost thoughts to the outside world. These sometimes come as a surprise especially, one feels, to the player when he reads them next morning in cold print.

Living and working for a week at a PGA European Tour event is like inhabiting a self-

A guest takes an early breakfast in one of the sponsor's hospitality tents.

Off the course the tented village always offers plenty to look at, and buy.

contained world which functions independently from everything else. The days are long and busy and entirely occupied by making sure the tournament runs smoothly. And at a venue like St Pierre, where hotel accommodation is provided on site, there is little need to leave the course.

During the week one does scan the newspapers, but only for coverage of the tournament; and there is little time to relax in front of the television. It is only when one drives out of the gate on Monday morning that one again becomes conscious of the real world outside. The bubble of the time capsule is punctured and, as the stands and pavilions come down, thoughts turn to other things and the circus moves on to yet another tournament.

THE MAJORS

British Open

The British Open is the oldest surviving golf tournament in the world, having first been played in 1860 at Prestwick. Although the term 'Open' is normally given to tournaments in which amateurs and professionals are allowed, this first 'Open' was restricted purely to professionals.

The start to such a great tournament was rather inauspicious with only eight professionals taking part over the 12-hole seaside course on the Ayrshire coast. The winner that first year was Willie Park from Musselburgh, beating the local hero Tom Morris Senior by two strokes over 36 holes. Although born at St Andrews, 'Old Tom', as he was forever known, had become the club professional at Prestwick in 1851, albeit without any formal salary. Professionals in those days only earned what they won on wagers by winning golf matches, or by tending the greens.

Over the next ten years Willie Park and the Morris family fought it out for the winner's leather belt, Old Tom gaining revenge in 1861 and 1862.

In 1868 'Young' Tom Morris, then 17 years old, took over the mantle from his four-times winning father, in the process gaining the first recorded hole-in-one at the 145-yard eighth at Prestwick. In 1870 Young Tom won the Open for the third time, and as three-times winners were entitled to keep the belt, he decided he really would; so 1871 saw no competition, there being no prize!

The astonished organisers at the Prestwick club, together with the Honourable Company of Edinburgh Golfers and the Royal and Ancient Golf Club, put up a trophy as a replacement – the famous silver jug still competed for today – for 1872. Young Tom Morris went straight out and won that too!

Having spent its first decade at Prestwick, it was then time for the competition to move around, the advent of the railways having made travel over long distances so much easier; indeed, the railways played a huge part in the spread of golf. Yet it stayed in Scotland until 1894, rotating between Prestwick, Musselburgh and St Andrews until 1892 when the Honourable Company of Edinburgh Golfers moved from Musselburgh to their new

home at Muirfield. Fittingly, the last time it was held at Musselburgh, in 1889, Willie Park Junior won it, 29 years after his father had won that first tournament.

The year after, at Prestwick, saw the first victory by an Englishman, as John Ball from Liverpool became the first of only three amateurs ever to win the Open; Harold Hilton, who won twice, and the great Bobby Jones, who won three times, were the others.

After the 1891 tournament at St Andrews it was decided to change the format from 36 holes to 72, but the competition remained strokeplay.

In 1894 the Open came south of the border for the first time, to Royal St George's at Sandwich on the Kent coast. The winner that year – and the first English *professional* to win it – was the famous JH Taylor with a 72-hole score of 326. The following year he repeated his victory, knocking four strokes off his total over the Old Course at St Andrews. He went on to win it five times in all, one of four players to do so, the others being James Braid, Peter Thomson and Tom Watson.

The year after Taylor's second victory, a

A huge crowd surrounds the 18th green at Royal Birkdale as the 1991 Open approaches its climax.

A unique piece of golfing history at the 1990 Open at St Andrews as former champions pose in front of the R and A.

Lee Trevino, Open champion in 1971 (Birkdale) and 1972 (Muirfield).

Mark Calcavecchia, Open champion in 1989 at Troon.

Seve Ballesteros, champion in 1979 (Lytham) and 1984 (St Andrews) wins for a third time in 1988 at Lytham.

Sandy Lyle celebrates a birdie on his way to victory at Royal St Georges in 1985.

Tom Watson powered his way to five Open titles.

young man from Jersey won it at Muirfield with a score of 316 after a play-off. He went on to win it six times in all, a record never equalled. His name was Harry Vardon.

Until the First World War, Vardon was part of the 'Great Triumvirate' with Taylor and Braid, and the Open became virtually their property, their succession of victories only being spoilt by Sandy Herd in 1902, J White in 1904, Frenchman Arnoud Massy in 1907 and Ted Ray in 1912.

The Great War caused the Open to be cancelled until 1920. The inter-war years were dominated by some of the greatest names in golf: Bobby Jones, Walter Hagen, Tommy Armour and Gene Sarazen, all Americans, and the Englishman Henry Cotton, those five taking the trophy 11 times between them, Hagen winning four. It was Hagen, in 1922, who became the first American-born winner, though Jock Hutchison, a Scottish-American born in Scotland but then resident in the US and representing the Glenview club in Chicago, had won it in 1921.

The Second World War again brought the competition to a halt but in 1946 it resumed, appropriately, at St Andrews, with Sam Snead taking the title. From then until 1969 the locals had very little to cheer about as Americans, Australians, New Zealanders and South Africans took the jug back home. From 1949 to 1958 it became almost the exclusive preserve of South African Bobby Locke and Australian Peter Thomson, only Max Faulkner and Ben Hogan interfering with their successive victories. Thomson won four times between 1954 and 1958, only being interrupted by Bobby Locke in 1957.

The legendary Arnold Palmer first won in 1961 at Royal Birkdale, repeating his victory at Troon the following year in front of the largest crowd ever to have attended an Open, an estimated 40 000 turning out in blistering heat to cheer Arnie round. Palmer never won the coveted jug again, though this became one of his favourite tournaments. In turn he became one of the most popular players to regularly visit Britain. His last Open, in 1990, when sadly he missed the cut, provoked many a nostalgic tear.

In 1963 the first left-hander ever to win the claret jug triumphed at Lytham, the New Zealander Bob Charles beating Phil Rogers in a play-off. It

was in that year that a few changes began to be made to the tournament, at that time played over three days with every competitor needing to pre-qualify. A series of exemptions for past champions and other top players was introduced and in 1966 the Open was spread to four days rather than three. That year was also the first when prize-money topped £20 000, Jack Nicklaus winning for the first time, at Muirfield.

Nicklaus came second the following year and again in 1968 when he narrowly lost to Gary Player of South Africa. It was in 1969 that Tony Jacklin kept the cup at home for the first time in 18 years, winning at Lytham. That championship was unique in modern times in that no American finished higher than sixth; trailing Jacklin were Bob Charles of New Zealand, Peter Thomson of Australia, Roberto de Vicenzo of Argentina and Christy O'Connor of Ireland. It was to be a rare year indeed.

America then took over again with Tom Watson, Jack Nicklaus, Lee Trevino, Tom Weiskopf and Johnny Miller all adding their names to the list of famous men preceding them. Only Gary Player in 1974 interrupted a string of US victories.

Nicklaus' victory in 1970 was achieved in true superman form. He was rather fortunate to be in a play-off with fellow American Doug Sanders, a pre-qualifier, as only Sanders' careless three-putting on the 72nd allowed Nicklaus another chance. He took it at the 18th, driving straight over the Swilken Bridge through the back of the green, a shot of well over 350 yards. A chip and a seven-foot putt finished it.

Trevino, in 1972, conjured up one of those devastating recovery shots to put himself in front of the leader, Tony Jacklin. It took the heart out of Jacklin and won Trevino his second Open. Nicklaus was again second, one of seven occasions on which he has finished runner-up.

The first Spaniard to win, Severiano Ballesteros, won his first in 1979 before Watson added another three victories. Seve won two more, in 1984 and 1988. The only Scot to win since 1910, Sandy Lyle, ironically had to do it south of the border at Sandwich in 1985, squeezed between Seve and Greg Norman, both of whom won in Scotland.

Nick Faldo landed his first victory at Muirfield in 1987, winning again – and pocketing £90 000 – in 1990 at a wonderful tournament at St Andrews in glorious weather. Faldo finished at the head of a field of almost 1500 players, though pre-qualifying tournaments brought that down to a realistic first-day total of 153.

The following year, 1991, has gone down as Australian year, with Ian Baker-Finch clinching the title from fellow Australian Mike Harwood. Another Aussie, the popular Craig Parry who had won the Bell's Scottish Open just a couple of weeks previously, came in eighth. Baker-Finch played inspired golf over the last two days. Sharing the lead going into the final round, he destroyed the opposition with five birdies in the first seven holes and coasted home with two shots to spare.

But perhaps the unluckiest player in 1991 was Richard Boxall who, just three shots off the lead on Saturday afternoon, broke his leg on the ninth tee, putting him out of golf until early 1992. He did receive a cheque for £3000 though, which was more than most of the original 1500 entrants got. A hundred years earlier there had been 40 entrants and the prize was a leather belt!

Spectators rush up the 18th at St Andrews in 1990 to see Nick Faldo putt out to win the Open.

US Masters

By the summer of 1930 Bobby Jones was the most celebrated and successful golfer in the world – and still an amateur. It came as a major shock then, when, having won the British Open at Hoylake with a score of 291, he sailed home to the States, won the US Open at Interlachen, Minnesota, with a 287, and promptly retired from golf. He was 28 years old.

It was his desire to establish an invitational golf tournament for his golfing friends and he found a course on which to hold it: Augusta National, a course designed by Dr Alister Mackenzie, with Jones' help, during the mid-1920s.

The Masters, as the tournament is still known (the name was given to the tournament to imply that only the top golfers in the world could participate), is unique in golf in that it is played on the same course every year. It is an invitational event, no player taking part unless invited by the organisers. In reality, all past winners at Augusta and recent winners of the other majors receive an invitation as do several other players, including the reigning Amateur champions of both the USA and Britain.

The first 'Masters' was held in 1934 with Bobby Jones himself playing though he could only manage 13th place well behind the first winner, Horton Smith. Smith won again in 1936 but in between came a famous victory carved out of a more famous shot.

On the 15th, a 500-yard par five, Gene Sarazen (who, incidentally, formally drove from the first tee to open the 1991 Masters for the last time, at the age of almost 90) was three shots off the lead when he hit his drive down the right side of the fairway. Left with 235 yards to the pin, Sarazen hit a four-wood over the water protecting the green and an amazed crowd watched the ball pitch at the front, roll tantalisingly up to the pin and drop for an albatross! That put him level with the leader Craig Wood and Sarazen went on to win the play-off the next day.

The unfortunate Wood, runner-up in 1934, had also narrowly lost the British Open in 1933 and the final of the 1934 US PGA (matchplay) and

was to lose the play-off in the US Open in 1939. By 1941 his luck had changed and he won both the Masters and the US Open.

The war brought a temporary halt to the tournament but in the last three years before the break the winning score was the same, 280, a score that has won no fewer than ten times in all. In 1947 Jimmy Demaret won for the second time and went on to become the first man to gain three victories by triumphing in 1950, coming from five strokes behind with six to play to win by two!

The king of them all: Jack Nicklaus walks off the 13th green at Augusta, where he has won the Masters a record six times.

Through the fifties the familiar, famous names of golf won the Masters: Arnold Palmer four times, Sam Snead three times and Ben Hogan twice. They were joined by the first non-American in 1961 when Gary Player won the coveted green jacket (which is worn by members only and thus classifies the winner as an honorary life member

No, not the mid-week seniors medal. Gene Sarazen and Sam Snead play in a curtain-raiser to the 1990 Masters.

of Augusta). It was the first of three victories for Player.

His first victory was very narrow though, only one ahead of Palmer and just two better than an amateur, Charlie Coe. Coming up the last, Player and Palmer were level and both drove into a bunker on the left of the fairway. Player achieved par; Palmer took a six.

In 1963 a young man (then 23 years old) won with a score of 286. Two years later he won it again with a record low score of 271, nine ahead of Palmer and Player, and then went on to become the first man ever successfully to defend the title, winning in 1966 (after a play-off) with the second-highest winning score ever, 288 (Sam Snead took 289 to win in 1954). The young man's name was Jack Nicklaus.

Perhaps the saddest end to a tournament came in 1968 when Roberto de Vicenzo of Argentina, who had won the British Open the previous summer, began his final round in brilliant form with an eagle and two birdies, going on to finish in 65 which tied him with Bob Goalby. His playing partner, marking his card, put him down for a four on the 17th and Roberto signed the card. Hundreds watching on television had clearly seen him take a three, yet the card was in and signed and could not be changed, despite appeals to Bobby Jones to intervene. The great old man refused – correctly. Vicenzo was never to win the Masters. It was the unkindest birthday present for de Vicenzo, 45 that very day.

Nicklaus won again in 1972 to equal Palmer's four victories, but Jack went on to add two more, in 1975 and 1986, the latter as the oldest ever winner at 46. He had been the youngest, too, but that record was beaten in 1980 by Severiano Ballesteros, two months younger than Jack had been for his first victory in 1963, when Seve had been only six years old! Nicklaus came second four times, too, as had Ben Hogan. Tom Weiskopf, who was never to win, also reached the runner-up position four times.

Ballesteros was the first European to win in 1980 and that victory proved to be the watershed for the 'European decade'. Seve added a second victory in 1983 and was followed by Germany's Bernhard Langer in 1985, Scotland's Sandy Lyle in 1988 and England's Nick Faldo in 1989. Faldo

Nick Faldo holes the longest ever putt at Augusta for a birdie at the second in 1989.

Sandy Lyle plays the shot of the decade from a bunker to set up his 1988 victory.

then became only the second man ever successfully to defend his title in 1990, with Welshman Ian Woosnam making it four in a row for Europe in 1991.

Lyle's 1988 victory must go down as one of the most dramatic. The Scot began the last round two shots ahead of Ben Crenshaw and Mark Calcavecchia. By the 16th tee he was two down to Calcavecchia, Crenshaw having faded. Lyle birdied that hole and was level after the 17th. Calcavecchia, playing ahead, got a safe four at the last and felt sure he had won when Lyle, hitting a one-iron off the 18th tee for safety, fired it straight into the bunker on the left of the fairway and 140 yards short of the pin. Recovery seemed impossible.

But not to Lyle. He hit a seven-iron from the bunker, cleared the second bunker by the front of the green and although the ball landed 20 feet past the flag the vast amount of backspin on the ball

Lyle putts out on the 18th green and the US Masters title is his. He celebrates with the now-famous jig.

screwed it back to within 10 feet. Lyle putted it for a birdie – and took the green jacket.

Faldo's victory in 1989 was equally momentous. Until the last round he had not played good golf. Thunderstorms on the third day had interrupted play and Faldo found it difficult to get into gear – until Sunday. He then went round in a superb 65 whilst the other contenders, including

Ballesteros and Norman, fell by the wayside. At the end Faldo's 283 was equalled by only one man, Scott Hoch.

Hoch and Faldo went into a sudden-death play-off. Both achieved par at the 10th, though Faldo had bunkered his approach and left himself a difficult putt. Hoch, normally a fast player on the green, stood over a two-foot putt for what seemed

An avid Masters spectator proudly displays tickets from previous years on his hat.

an age before missing it. They moved on to the 11th where Faldo hit a superb tee-shot, then left himself a 25-foot putt with Hoch not on the green. Faldo holed that in the early evening gloom for his first ever victory.

The following year, 1990, Faldo was back and in contention to become only the second man ever to win twice in succession. Ironically, he played his final round with the only other man ever to have done that, Jack Nicklaus.

It should have been Ray Floyd's day, though. He led by five at the start of the last day only to let that slide away, a bogey on 17 pulling him back to level with Faldo. Faldo had finished with a par on the last and sat quietly by the scorer's tent, waiting as Floyd came up the fairway.

The American's tee-shot found 'Lyle's bunker' on the left, 170 yards from the pin, from which he got close enough to make par and force

a play-off for the second year running. At the first play-off hole, the 485-yard par four 10th, Faldo bunkered his approach whilst Floyd was left with a 15-foot putt. Faldo hit a sand iron inside Floyd, to four feet for a safe par, matched by Floyd.

On the 11th again, the game was decided when Floyd hit his second shot, a seven-iron, into the lake on the left of the green. Faldo took an eight-iron to 25 feet and almost holed the long putt. It was all over.

Woosnam's 1991 victory produced an equally tense finish, the Welshman playing solid golf to get to the 18th tee level with Spain's José Maria Olazabal and America's Tom Watson.

Olazabal took a five on the last; so did Watson. But Woosnam, driving way left beyond the bunkers and most of the crowd swarming alongside the 18th fairway, held his nerve and made a four for a famous victory.

US Open

In 1895 the first official US Open was held at Newport, Rhode Island, on the east coast of the United States. Eleven players took part in a 36-hole competition, the winner being Horace Rawlins from the Isle of Wight, England.

There had been an unofficial event the previous year but as the US Golf Association was only founded in 1895, that earlier 'Open' can hardly count. For the record, it was won by Willie Dunn from Musselburgh who beat a fellow member of the Honourable Company of Edinburgh Golfers in the 'final'.

Indeed the first 14 years saw British winners, most of them expatriates who had sailed the Atlantic in search of a new life in the new land. Whether they can, in the strictest sense, be termed 'British' winners is open to debate.

For the first three years the tournament was won by expatriate Scots, even after it changed to

72 holes in 1898, in line with the British Open. At that time several of the leading British players were regularly touring America, proof of the enormous influence British golf had in the United States and proof also that sponsorship is far from being just a modern aspect of the game. In 1900 both Harry Vardon and JH Taylor were touring the US and both were in Chicago for the US Open that year, Vardon beating 'JH' by two shots. The third-placed golfer was 15 shots behind Vardon! Such was the supremacy of British golf then.

Willie Anderson, from North Berwick, ruled for the next five years, winning in 1901 and again in 1903, 1904 and 1905. Sadly, he died at the age of 30 a couple of years later.

At last, in 1911, the United States produced its first home-grown winner, Jimmy McDermott, a postman's son from Chicago. At 19 he was the youngest player ever to win the US Open and his

The US Open trophy. Many fine golfers have held the handsome cup . . .

. . . including Byron Nelson (1939) and Tom Watson (1982), pictured here together in 1990.

record still stands. To prove it wasn't just some fluke he retained the title the following year. Tragically, this fine young golfer's life was in ruins just three years later after he lost heavily on the stock market and was involved in a shipwreck on his way home from the British Open – where he failed to qualify. He played no golf after he was 23, even though he lived until 1972.

By this time the Americans were firmly in the driving seat and it was the turn of some amateurs to show their mettle, the young Francis Ouimet taking the 1913 title, beating Vardon by five shots. England's Ted Ray was third.

Two more amateurs won in 1915 and 1916 as the shadow of war loomed large over Europe and few golfers travelled westwards across the Atlantic. Walter Hagen had won his first title in 1914 and took the first peacetime title again in 1919 before Ted Ray came back to win his only title in 1920, beating Vardon into second place again. Cornish-born Jim Barnes won in 1921 but then it was time for true Americans to rule supreme.

The American run of successes, which was to last unbroken until 1965, began in 1922 with Eugene Saraceni, a 20-year-old man from New York State who stood just 5ft 5in tall. He went on to win all four of the majors before 1935. Saraceni, of obvious Italian descent, had changed his name at 17 to the more American name by which we know him: Gene Sarazen. His final round of 68 in 1922 was the lowest then recorded in the US Open. At the beginning of that round he had not even been in contention. He went on to win the US PGA a few months later.

Then came the man Sarazen had beaten into second place, Bobby Jones. He won in 1923, 1926 (when he also won the British Open) and 1929. Then came the incredible year of 1930 when he won his Grand Slam (British and US Opens, British and US Amateurs). Sarazen copied half of Jones' success two years later by winning both the US and British Opens. As a professional, of course, he could not enter the other two.

The growth in golf in the United States was demonstrated by the fact that 1930 saw over 100 entries for the competition, professionals and amateurs from every part of the US entering for the pre-qualifying rounds.

It was not until 1939 that another American hero took over the superstar banner. Although Byron Nelson won the Open only once, his impact

The evening shadows lengthen at Hazeltine (1991) as another day of US Open golf draws to a close.

on American golf went far beyond his numerous tournament victories. He was the role model for many young American golfers, including the man who was to become the next folk hero of American golf, a fellow Texan, Ben Hogan.

In 1948 when Hogan won for the first time, setting a new low record of 276, he was 36 and had only really broken into the big time eight years earlier. After winning the US Open, he, like Sarazen, went on to take the US PGA later in the year, a title Hogan had also claimed two years previously. He won the US Open again in 1950, 1951 and 1953, that last year as a double winner as he also took the British Open.

Arnold Palmer, having just won the Masters, arrived in 1960 looking confident. At the start of the last round he was seven shots off the lead, but in one of the late surges for which he became famous – and feared by all other players – he took six birdies on the first seven holes to win by two from a young amateur named Jack Nicklaus. Two years later Nicklaus, then a professional, had his revenge, beating Palmer in a play-off. Jack has won four US Open titles.

The sixties and seventies saw Nicklaus come along regularly to win, accompanied by Lee Trevino, Hale Irwin and, in 1965, the first non-American to win for many decades, Gary Player, who promptly gave $25000 of the prize money back to the USGA for cancer relief and the promotion of junior golf. There was another non-American win in 1970, from England's Tony Jacklin – the first British winner since Ted Ray 50 years earlier – by a record-beating seven shots. Eleven years later, in between Trevino, Nicklaus and Irwin again, another non-US player won, Australia's David Graham, though at that time he was living and playing full-time in America.

Since then the winners' list has read like a roll of honour of modern American greats – Tom Watson, Larry Nelson, Fuzzy Zoeller, Ray Floyd, Scott Simpson and, in both 1988 and 1989, Curtis Strange, only the sixth man to win back-to-back in the US Open.

His first victory came in an exciting finish. Nick Faldo had led the field for some time on the last day and looked like clinching the title but Strange had other ideas and recovered brilliantly with a last-gasp bunker shot on the 72nd to tie. Strange then won the play-off.

The next year was no easier with Strange the only leading player to complete a level-par final

The 1989 hole-in-one clan. All four players, incredibly, aced the same hole (the sixth) on the same day (day two). All used seven-irons. Left to right: Tom Weaver, Jerry Pate, Nick Price, Mark Weibe.

One US Open champion, Jerry Pate (1976), interviews another, Curtis Strange, after the 1988 event at Brookline.

round as Tom Kite and Scott Simpson fell away. Then in 1990 came the oldest ever winner at 45 years old, and a man who had first won this tournament 26 years previously, before most of the 4000 original entrants had been born: Hale Irwin.

In 1991, after the first day was disrupted by heavy rain and thunderstorms during which one spectator was killed, the European challenge faded after the second day. The tournament, played at the Hazeltine course in Minnesota where Jacklin had won his US Open in 1970, proved very difficult, only six players breaking par for their four rounds. Jack Nicklaus commented that the rough, just off the fairway, was so long that any stray shots were severely punished.

The tournament ended in drama with a putt at the last levelling the scores at six under for Scott Simpson and Payne Stewart. In the 18-hole Monday play-off, Payne Stewart won by two. Although trailing at the 15th, he played safe, solid golf through the last three holes whilst Simpson let a missed putt on the 16th get to him so much that he missed the short 17th green completely and looked a beaten man even before he reached the 18th tee.

Strange gets up and down from this bunker by the 17th on his way to that victory.

Curtis hugs the trophy at Oak Hill having retained it in 1989 with a 278 – the same as his winning score the previous year.

US PGA

Although regarded as the least important of the four 'majors', the US PGA Tournament is the third oldest, having been started in 1916, the year the United States Professional Golfers' Association (USPGA) was founded. The fledgling USPGA wanted a tournament especially for its own members, many years before all professional golfers became members of the Association. Until 1957 it was played as a matchplay tournament, leading to some exciting head-to-head battles over the years.

The first winner – before a two-year break as America entered the Great War – was Jim Barnes, originally from Cornwall. He beat a Scottish-American, Jock Hutchison, by one hole. Barnes went on to win both the US and British Opens after the war as well as the US PGA again in 1919.

The first big name to win the championship was Walter Hagen in 1921 when he beat Barnes 3 and 2. Hagen handed over his crown to Gene Sarazen the next year but after losing to Sarazen

in 1923 he came roaring back to win four titles in a row from 1924 to 1927. Although Jack Nicklaus has since equalled his five wins (though at strokeplay, after the format changed in 1958), the record has not yet been beaten.

Sarazen's victory in 1923 had its moments of drama and a hint of sourness as Sarazen, attempting to cut a corner on the second extra play-off hole, hooked into woods, his ball bouncing off the roof of a cottage. Sarazen's caddie found the ball sitting up with a perfect view of the green, which Sarazen proceeded to hit. Hagen, astounded at Sarazen's 'luck' in finding the ball in such a good position, floundered and missed his approach. He was ever

afterwards convinced someone had moved the ball, but there was no proof either way.

Sarazen went on to win again in 1933, but before that, in both 1928 and 1929, Leo Diegel, the man who never thought he would win a major (he had led the US Open in 1920 by three with five to go but proceeded to drop four strokes in the next three to come second) had two fine victories, by 6 and 5 and 6 and 4. He had ended Hagen's run in the third round before crushing Sarazen 9 and 8 in the semi-final in the first of his victorious years. The 1929 final was memorable for the fact that his opponent, Johnny Farrell, twice knocked Diegel's ball into the hole, this at a time when you did not lift your ball on the green but had to play round or over stymies – rather like snookers in the table-top game.

Tommy Armour, Byron Nelson and Sam Snead all added their names to the list of winners before a one-year break in 1943 owing to the Second World War. But most of the other winners were not internationally known names, rather journeyman professionals playing regularly on the US tour – exactly what the founding fathers of the tournament would have wished.

The largest winning margin came in 1938 when Paul Runyon beat Sam Snead 8 and 7, Runyon having won previously in 1934, that time only edging ahead on the 38th hole.

So it continued after the war, with players whose names are barely still remembered – Ferrier, Harper, Harbert, Burkemo, Ford and Rosburg – though some of golf's legends have added this title to their impressive catalogue of victories. Nelson and Snead again, Ben Hogan in 1946 and 1948, and more recently the more recognisable names of Nicklaus, Trevino, Floyd, Wadkins, Player and Stockton have all been winners.

In 1958 the decision was taken to change to strokeplay, like the other major tournaments, that format being considered more in keeping with professional golf at the time, particularly as a spectator and television sport where the matches went all the way to the 18th green. In matchplay they could be finished by the 12th, thus robbing

Steve Richardson and David Feherty lead the European challenge at Crooked Stick in 1991. No European has ever won the US PGA.

spectators and television audiences the opportunity of seeing the 'winning putt' on the 18th as a grand climax.

Interestingly, the first winner in strokeplay format, Dow Finsterwald, had been the beaten finalist the previous year, at matchplay. Finsterwald was, at that time, regarded as the best American hope for the future and played four times in the Ryder Cup, but the arrival of Arnold Palmer eclipsed his rising stardom. He never won another major, though he had many US tour victories.

1962 saw the first foreign player to win under the new format, Gary Player, with a 278 over the four rounds, two years before he went on to win the US Open. In that PGA win he defeated Bob Goalby, the man who was to snatch the Masters victory from Roberto de Vicenzo in 1968, by a stroke. The year after saw Jack Nicklaus, who had won the Masters earlier that year at Augusta, take the title in his second year as a professional, one of five wins in this event. He has also finished second more times than anyone else, having four runner-up placings.

David Graham, the popular Australian who was, by then, a US resident and a player on the American tour, claimed the first 'Aussie' win in 1979, yet no British player has won in modern times (Jim Barnes was the last, in 1916 and 1919, though he was living in the US), lacking primarily the time spent on the US tour to qualify for inclusion; although several, including Nick Faldo, had played on the US tour before the European tour became big enough (and rich enough) to keep them at home during the summer months.

The 1986 championship at Toledo, Ohio, has gone down as a classic, primarily because of the continuing battle between Bob Tway and Greg Norman, another Australian resident in the United States. Norman, fresh from his victory in the British Open at Turnberry, started by setting a new course record of 65. Tway began relatively poorly but then, in the third round, reduced the course record to 64.

On the last day they played together, being neck and neck to the 17th when Tway hit the rough round the green, yet still managed to get up and down for par. On the 18th Norman thought his luck had changed, being on the green in regulation whilst Tway was in a bunker. Tway

saved it by holing his sand shot and beat Norman into second place.

Payne Stewart, a popular player on both sides of the Atlantic, won his first major title in 1989, a year before coming second to Faldo in the British Open at St Andrews. In that year, American Mike Reid was cruising to victory in both the Masters and the PGA but threw both away in a few moments of last-minute madness. Australian Wayne Grady took the 1990 title in an uninspiring event but that was reversed in 1991 by the literally last-minute arrival of a young man from Memphis, Tennessee, as John Daly's big hitting won him the event by three clear strokes. Thus the man who was ninth reserve and had only found out he was playing hours before he teed off, now found his name on the famous cup alongside those of Nicklaus, Sarazen, Hogan, Nelson and Snead

Enough to make a grown man cry! Payne Stewart's tears of joy – and perhaps relief – after his 1989 victory.

Right: *A fairy-tale come true – John Daly came through from eighth reserve to win by a mile at Crooked Stick, 1991.*

INTERNATIONAL TOURNAMENTS

Ryder Cup

In 1912 Abe Mitchell, a golfer from Forest Row in Sussex, close to what is now Gatwick airport, was beaten in a play-off for the British Amateur Championship at Westward Ho!. Mitchell received considerable praise for his play and decided to turn professional. In 1926 he played in a hastily arranged, unofficial 'international' match between British and American professionals at Wentworth, beating the reigning US Open champion Jim Barnes 8 and 7, then teaming up with George Duncan to beat Barnes and Walter Hagen 9 and 8.

In the crowd that day was Samuel Ryder, a market gardener from Cheshire who had moved south to establish a seeds business. Ryder persuaded Mitchell to become his personal golf tutor and, thrilled by the prospect of international matches, suggested that a regular Britain versus America

tournament should be established. He put up a gold trophy (which cost £250 and is surmounted by the figure of Abe Mitchell, in honour of his tutor) and the Ryder Cup was in progress.

The following year, 1927, a British team led by Ted Ray and including George Duncan sailed to New York, funded primarily by public subscription, to take part in the first tournament. Their opponents were captained by Walter Hagen. Jim Farrell, Leo Diegel, Gene Sarazen and Joe Turnesa were in the American side which walked out easy winners by 9½ to 2½. The visiting side scored only one point in the foursomes; the only singles points came from George Duncan who beat Joe Turnesa by one hole over 36 and Charles Whitcombe who halved with Gene Sarazen.

The following tournament (the Ryder Cup

An emotional finish at the Belfry in 1985 brought the Ryder Cup to Europe for the first time in 28 years. Tony Jacklin receives the trophy.

The underdog wins! Ireland's David Feherty, playing his first Ryder Cup, beats US Open champion Payne Stewart in the singles in 1991.

So near yet so far. The European players living on their nerves as Bernhard Langer fights valiantly to save the day in the last singles match, 1991 . . .

. . . to no avail! The USA win back the trophy and captain Dave Stockton embraces Hale Irwin at the end of his epic battle with Langer.

is played for biennially) in 1929 was at Leeds and here the British team had its revenge, George Duncan beating the great Walter Hagen 10 and 8 – still the largest singles victory in a Ryder Cup match.

On that occasion Abe Mitchell did play, though losing in his singles match 9 and 8 to Leo Diegel. Young Henry Cotton won his first match, too, by 4 and 3, that point being the decider.

The next three tournaments went with home advantage; America, with Hagen, Sarazen, Espinosa, Farrell and Diegel, won 9–3 in Columbus, Ohio, in temperatures which climbed above 100 degrees, and Britain, captained by the great JH Taylor and literally knocked into shape by a PT instructor who had the team running along Southport beach at dawn, crept home by a single point in 1933; America also triumphed in New Jersey in 1935, again by the large margin of 9–3. That year was historic in that it saw the British side fielding three brothers, the Whitcombes, though they only managed one point between them.

In 1937, a year after Sam Ryder died, Walter Hagen, captaining a US side for the last time, brought his team, which included Sarazen, Snead, Byron Nelson and Ralph Guldahl, to Southport. Britain included Dai Rees, Cotton and

Percy Alliss. There was no running along the sands this time and perhaps it showed because the Americans gained the first 'away' victory in the series, by 8 points to 4.

War interfered with proceedings for 10 years after that, the next match being played in November 1947 at Portland, Oregon. The years of deprivation and rationing had had their effect on the visitors who went down 11–1. Two years later the scores were closer at Ganton, Scarborough, when an American team captained by Ben Hogan won 7–5. The beautiful Pinehurst resort in North Carolina was the scene for the 1951 confrontation. Hogan, Snead and Demaret helped the home side to a stunning 9–2 victory.

Wentworth hosted the 1953 match which came to an end in high drama, with young Peter Alliss losing his match on the final hole and Bernard Hunt, playing for the first time, only managing a half when he should have cruised to victory. America won 6½–5½.

The 1955 match in California went the home side's way, as was expected, but then came 1957 at Lindrick, Yorkshire. The Americans won the foursomes 3–1 but then lost out heavily in the singles as Christy O'Connor, Dai Rees, Eric Brown and Bernard Hunt all won their matches against an American team containing names hardly

now remembered. It was enough, though; Britain and Ireland won comfortably by three clear points.

A return visit to California in the November sunshine of 1959 saw the Americans take back the Cup they were now believing was theirs by right. By the time of the next match the format had been changed, the foursomes and singles being cut from 36 holes to 18. America still won, though.

In 1963 at Atlanta, Georgia, another change took place, fourball matches being introduced for the first time. Neil Coles, Hunt, Alliss, O'Connor and Brian Huggett were on the losing side as the Americans, with Arnold Palmer, Julius Boros, Gene Littler, Billy Casper and Tony Lema, romped to a 23–9 victory. Royal Birkdale hosted the 1965 match but again a strong American side dominated and duly returned home with the trophy. It stayed there after the 1967 match in Houston, Texas.

Two years later, in 1969, the contest was

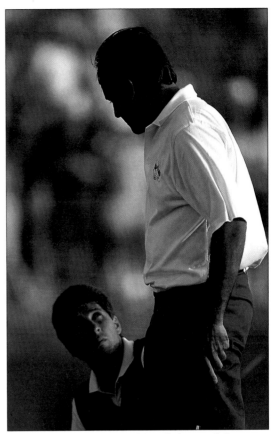

Spain's Ballesteros and Olazabal one of the most successful Ryder Cup partnerships ever, often holding the European side together.

Above: *Jacklin and co. celebrate holding onto the Ryder Cup after the tie at the Belfry in 1989.*

Right: *Tom Kite and Curtis Strange study the line of a putt together at the Belfry in 1989.*

back at Royal Birkdale. At the end of the second day it was all square, with 12 of the 16 matches going to the last hole and none of them ending before the 16th. The last day began with singles

Never smile at a crocodile . . . Nick Faldo in fact had little to smile about at Kiawah Island in 1991 – he gained just one point, beating Ray Floyd in the final day's singles.

wins in the morning for Coles, O'Connor, Maurice Bembridge, Peter Butler and Tony Jacklin. Trevino, Hill and Casper got three back for the USA.

In the afternoon the US dominated, Britain's only two wins coming from Butler and Bernard Gallacher. The penultimate match between Huggett and Casper was halved. Out on the course was the last match, Nicklaus against Jacklin.

On the par-five 17th, Nicklaus was one up and on the green in two with a possible chance of a birdie. Jacklin, who had won the British Open a few months earlier, was also on the green – and holed an eagle putt of over 30 feet to square the match. The entire result now rested on the final hole. History records that Nicklaus, who had lost to Jacklin that morning by 4 and 3, conceded a putt of three feet that was by no means a certainty. That sporting gesture from one of the world's best

golfers halved not only the match but the entire contest.

Nicklaus would further change the history of the Ryder Cup by persuading the golfing powers to allow the British and Irish team to be expanded to bring in some of the more promising players from other countries in Europe, particularly Spain. That change did not take effect for a few years, though. In the meantime the United States held on to the trophy, but Brian Barnes deserves a mention as the only man ever to beat Jack Nicklaus twice in one day, in 1975.

It was in 1979 that the match became the United States of America versus Europe. In came Seve Ballesteros, Bernhard Langer, José Maria Canizares, Manuel Pinero, José Rivero and Antonio Garrido. But still America prevailed, with Tom Watson, Curtis Strange, Craig Stadler, Ben

Crenshaw and Lanny Wadkins victorious.

Then came 1985 at the Belfry in England. Two years before, Europe had come within a point of a tie, captained by Tony Jacklin. This time the Europeans, enjoying home advantage, were cheered on by a huge crowd and in the final afternoon's singles Sam Torrance curled a long putt on the 18th to beat Hal Sutton and win the Cup for Europe.

Interest in the US, which had waned with continued victories, was rekindled, and the 1987 event at Murifield Village, Ohio, a course designed by Nicklaus, was attended by a huge crowd. After two days Europe were 10–3 in the lead and although the Americans came back in the final day's singles it was not enough. Europe won 13–11.

Back at the Belfry in 1989, expectations were high; but America had a very strong team and stormed into a commanding lead. Europe fought back and it was left to Christy O'Connor Jnr to fire a two-iron across the water at the 18th to snatch victory and assure a tie, thus keeping the Cup in Europe for the third successive time, the longest period of sustained European predominance.

The alligator-infested wetlands of South Carolina's Kiawah Island seemed an unlikely venue for the 1991 confrontation, but the US golf architect Pete Dye created a dramatic and testing course out of sand dunes that were devasted by Hurricane Hugo halfway through construction. The venue was to have been somewhere in California but prime-time television schedules dictated that the East Coast it must be.

The European side, with five 'rookies' – Colin Montgomerie, David Gilford, Steve Richardson, Paul Broadhurst and David Feherty – arrived with the Cup in Concorde, swooping low over the course on their approach to Charleston airport. The USA, roared on by a huge crowd of 40 000 each day, stormed into the lead but were pulled back each afternoon, the teams going into the Sunday singles all square.

Steve Pate, injured in a car accident earlier in the week, withdrew, leaving David Gilford without a match. The points on that were sportingly halved. Faldo, Ballesteros, Broadhurst and Feherty all won, the latter beating America's top player, US Open champion Payne Stewart, 2 and 1. Colin

A tie at the Belfry gives both captains, Tony Jacklin and Ray Floyd, the chance to hold the trophy – though it was Europe that retained it.

Montgomerie came back from five down to halve his match with Mark Calcavecchia on the last.

But for the United States, Paul Azinger, Corey Pavin, Fred Couples, Lanny Wadkins and Chip Beck all recorded victories in their matches. The outcome hung on the last match, between 46-year-old Hale Irwin and Germany's Bernhard Langer.

Langer, needing to win to retain the Cup for Europe, came back from two down at the 15th, winning both the 16th and the devastatingly difficult 17th – a 200-yard par three with a carry across a lake to a narrow green, which Langer had aced in a practice round earlier in the week. They went down the 18th neck and neck, both were just off the green in two. Langer was well inside Irwin's poor chip in three, but missed his putt to win the match, the ball nudging the edge of the hole but failing to drop. The match was halved – America regained the trophy by one point and the European side climbed back on Concorde without having to complete any customs declaration forms for silverware!

Bernard Gallacher found his first Ryder Cup as European captain a baptism of fire.

Langer's putt shaves the hole on the 18th against Hale Irwin. Had it dropped, the Cup would have returned with the European team on Concorde.

Curtis Cup

The Curtis Cup, played for by lady amateurs, can trace its origins back a full quarter-century before even the Ryder Cup began. It was in 1905 that two American sisters, Harriet and Margaret Curtis, sailed over to England to play in the British Women's Amateur at Cromer in Norfolk. The reigning champion, Lottie Dod, arranged an impromptu 'international' the day before the real tournament began. No result was recorded, but the Curtis sisters were so thrilled at playing that they decided to launch an international team tournament for lady golfers 'of all lands'. In reality it became a biennial match between the United States and Great Britain/Ireland.

Nothing much happened for a few years and it was not until 1930 that a further unofficial match took place at Sunningdale. Two years later,

with the blessing of the golf authorities on both sides of the Atlantic, the Curtis Cup began, a beautiful silver bowl having been provided as the trophy for the winning side. America won the first match 5½–3½ with players of the quality of Glenna Collett for the US and Joyce Wethered and Diana Fishwick for Britain and Ireland.

Apart from a tie in 1936 at Gleneagles, the Americans were dominant and it was not until 1952 that the British team won, curiously at Muirfield where the Honourable Company of Edinburgh Golfers had no lady members, nor would they allow them the use of any club facilities. Jean Donald led the home side to victory on that famous course just a week after she had won the Scottish Ladies' title at Gullane, the course almost next door.

Great Britain and Ireland's victorious 1988 team at Sandwich celebrate their win by 11 points to 7.

The next British and Irish victory came four years later at Sandwich, when the home side won by 5 points to 4, an exact reversal of the score on the other side of the Atlantic two years earlier. At Sandwich the result hung on the very last match and that went to the final hole before a victory for Britain and Ireland was secured. Two years after that, near Boston, the sides finished level – the

Above: *June Thornhill scored 8 points out of a possible 12 in her three Cup appearances. A long putt at St Georges in 1988 helps the home side to victory.*

Left: *Britain's captain Diane Bailey receives the trophy in 1988.*

Stephens) was dormie up after 17 of the last match, needing to halve the 18th to draw level. She went one better, winning by two to record that little piece of history.

The best was yet to come, though. Despite the fact that the United States held on to the trophy for another quarter-century, 1986 saw a famous 'away' victory, Britain and Ireland winning in Kansas – the first British team victory in America by men or women, amateur or professional. Trish Johnson won all four of her matches for the visitors and Diane Bailey, as captain, played a significant part in a famous victory.

The trophy was retained in 1988 at Royal St George's in chilly, windy conditions which suited the Europeans more than their guests, but the United States had its revenge in 1990 by the considerable margin of 14–4, including a whitewash of the last day's singles, 6–0.

first time any British golf team, amateur or professional, had avoided defeat in America. Again the match went to the very last hole, Britain's Mrs Smith (the former Miss Frances

Walker Cup

Just after the First World War, a delegation from the US Golf Association sailed to Britain to discuss with the R and A the unifying of the rules of golf on both sides of the Atlantic. During their visit, the President of the USGA, George Herbert Walker, announced that he was donating a cup to be played for by teams of (amateur) 'golfers from all nations'.

Invitations were sent out to numerous countries asking if they would like to enter a team – sadly, none did.

In 1921 a number of American players set sail for England to take part in the British Amateur championship. Before the championship itself they played an unofficial 'team' match against the British players, winning comfortably by 9–3.

The following year, 1922, the R and A sent a British team to Long Island for the first match, but a strong home team, which included Bobby Jones and Francis Ouimet, romped home by 8 points to 4 in what was to become a long list of US victories, the most crushing of which were to come in 1928 at Chicago and 1961 at Seattle when the British side managed to win only one singles match in the entire event.

Until 1924 the matches were played annually but it was decided that this was too much of a strain, so there was a switch to alternate years, a formula followed by the Ryder Cup when it began a few years later.

In 1926 the match was at St Andrews where Bobby Jones, having just won the British Open at Royal Lytham, scored one of the largest singles victories ever, defeating Cyril Tolley 12 and 11 in what should have been a 36-hole match.

The next two matches went to the Americans too, by huge margins: 11–1 and 10–2. In 1930 Jones again had an important victory over Roger Wethered – brother of Joyce – by 9 and 8, to go with his other successes in that Grand Slam year. Perhaps the best battle of that match was between the American Don Moe and Britain's Bill Stout. In a 36-hole match Stout was seven up after 21 holes. Moe then won seven on the trot, finished with a birdie on the 36th and won the point.

In 1932 the Brits were almost whitewashed at Boston, the only point being won by Leonard Crawley. His other claim to fame is that he hit the trophy with a very wayward shot, putting quite a nasty dent in the side. Worse was to follow four years later at Pine Valley, New Jersey, when the visitors failed to win a single match.

Not until 1938, with the shadow of war hanging over Europe, did the British team snatch a victory, by one point at St Andrews. By then Bobby Jones, who won every match but one he ever played in the Walker Cup, had retired, but the Americans still had the stronger team, buoyed up, perhaps, by the fact that the college system in the United States gives more opportunities for competitive golf than the weekend medal habit back in Britain. Although this situation has changed in recent years, it is still a major contributing factor towards the success the Americans have enjoyed over the British in other sports, the most obvious other example being tennis. A strong American side descended on St Andrews in confident expectation of the match being just one more formality, but the home side won with several points to spare.

Peachtree, 1989. Jim Milligan is congratulated by his colleagues after his match against Jay Sigel brought victory to Britain and Ireland.

The victorious Britain and Ireland Walker Cup team of 1989.

The restart after the war was again at St Andrews in 1947, the Americans conceding home advantage out of respect, but they triumphed and continued to do so every other year until 1965 in Baltimore when the two teams were level, the only time there has been a tie.

Britain and Ireland won again at St Andrews in 1971 – a lucky venue, obviously – and by this time the formula had been changed to foursomes and singles, the matches being over just 18 holes rather the 36 as previously.

In 1973 America again had revenge, their victories being founded upon getting a good start in the foursomes, though losing ground in the singles. In recent times the matches have become more even, the Americans winning narrowly in 1985, by a huge margin in 1987, and in 1989 helping to produce a dramatic finish at Peachtree, Atlanta.

At lunch on the last day the British side was leading 11–5, but the Americans, in the afternoon's singles, went wild, fighting back to within one point, leaving the last match to decide the result.

With three to play, Britain's Jim Milligan, playing in his first Walker Cup, was two down to one of the best amateur golfers to come out of America in recent times, Jay Sigel. Birdies on the 16th and 17th put the match all square as they came down the last. Milligan stayed cool to halve the match – and win the Cup.

The American side gained revenge by 14–10 in 1991 at the Irish links course at Portmarnock in a rather unexciting finish, the match having been virtually decided on the first day as the Americans built up a huge lead.

By 1991, 25 Walker Cup players had gone on to represent their country in the Ryder Cup, 10 from Britain, 15 from the United States. These include, on the British side, Howard Clark, Gordon Brand, Mark James, Sandy Lyle, Peter Oosterhuis, Ronan Rafferty and Colin Montgomerie; the American ex-amateurs can boast Tom Kite, Gene Littler, Jack Nicklaus, Jerry Pate, Scott Simpson, Craig Stadler, Curtis Strange, Hal Sutton and Lanny Wadkins.

GOLF ON TELEVISION

WHEN Nick Faldo came marching up the 18th at St Andrews one summer Sunday in 1990 on his way to collecting his second British Open victory, a great crowd of spectators, each eager to see him putt out to win the historic claret jug, swarmed across the fairway just below the Valley of Sin.

A way was forced through the good-humoured crowd by assorted police and course marshals and he then calmly two-putted for a final round of 71 and a famous victory. There was, that glorious Sunday evening, a crowd estimated at anything between 20 000 and 40 000 at the home of golf, but it was nothing in comparison to the vast numbers watching that historic scene around the world.

They, though, were sitting comfortably at home – or perhaps elsewhere, as was the author, who was on a Lufthansa flight to Frankfurt but still watching on a portable television. In Britain over eight million people were watching Faldo that day, as were countless others in 22 countries worldwide.

Television coverage of golf has been, without doubt, one of the biggest factors in the growth of its popularity. Before television became involved, crowds were smaller and the game was more the preserve of the rich. Since regular TV coverage began in the 1970s, the number of people taking up the Royal and Ancient game has multiplied phenomenally.

Yet covering a major tournament such as the Open is not just a simple matter of turning up with a few cameras and the people behind the well-known voices of television commentary – mainly Peter Alliss, Alex Hay and Bruce Critchley in Britain. At the Open these three are supported by close to 300 others excluding catering and other outside support staff.

The planning for the four-day coverage of the Open begins 10 months earlier with a series of visits by the executive producer John Shrewsbury, producer/director Alastair Scott, engineering manager Peter Wright and one or two others. Their first visits are to plan the locations of each of the 20 cameras (with back-up support from three mobile cameras during the event) and to decide which greens, fairways and tees would be best covered.

At most courses, one camera will cover only one fairway or green. Often, though, what is termed 'camera migration' will be planned – a camera covering an early hole or perhaps the first tee will be moved to cover a closing green, entailing its physical transportation to another site and its hoisting into place and set-up, a process that can easily take an hour.

The prime concern at this early planning stage is to ensure that the cameras are in the best locations possible but do not interfere with the golf – having a camera in the way of a possible shot could prove costly to the golfer, to say nothing of the potentially disastrous implications for the cameraman perched on his scaffolding 20 feet above the fairway!

The R and A, or for other events the PGA European Tour, are obviously very heavily involved, as many other items of 'furniture' – grandstands, hospitality units, the tented village, catering facilities and so on – need to be given sufficient space. These all require power cables which must be easily accessible in case of a fault yet as unobtrusive as possible to the spectators who will turn up on the day.

For television cameras, line of sight is one of the prime concerns and the planners, often visiting the site in mid-winter, need to be aware of the potential growth of trees or shrubs which might, on that occasion, be bare. Nearer the time of the event all the logistics planning is completed, including the arrival times of all the paraphernalia that goes to make up an OB (outside broadcast) unit, the amount of cabling needed, the locations of all the fixed microphones, the accommodation for the crews, the erection of the scaffolding towers, a parking grid so that everything is put in

Above: *High cameras allow the armchair viewer to see almost any part of the course.*

Overleaf: *Planning the 'camera line' is vital – ideally they should see but not be seen.*

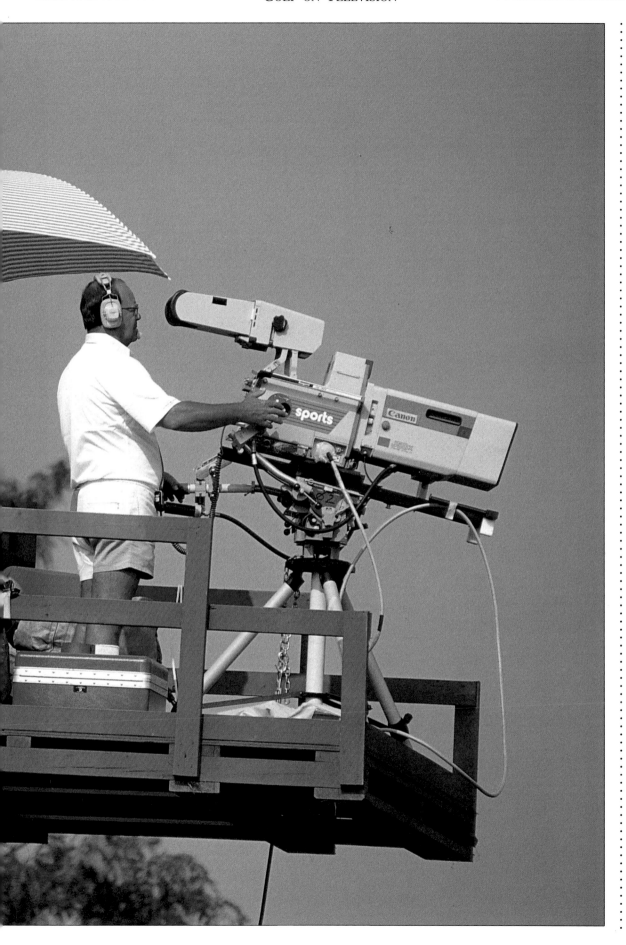

The cameraman on his lofty perch needs to be ready for any weather conditions.

the right spot, and not least, the total cost estimates for the coverage.

These vary from event to event, a smallish event like the Epson Grand Prix costing perhaps £180 000, rising to almost £500 000 for coverage of the Open. Some of that is recouped by selling coverage to overseas broadcasters.

On the Thursday before the tournament begins, cables are laid – an average of 50 miles of cables are put down just for television. By the weekend, the camera scaffold towers have been erected, trackway to take heavy vehicles has been laid, and the OB unit trailers are arriving.

British Telecom is heavily involved in supplying high quality telephone circuits to carry the signals from the course to television transmitters, though in some parts of the world direct satellite links are used, as happened for the BBC coverage of the 1991 Ryder Cup in South Carolina. From the Kiawah Island course BBC transmissions were sent by satellite to New York, then across the Atlantic via another satellite to the BBC transmitters before reaching the living rooms of an estimated six million viewers in Britain.

On Monday, before the players begin arriving, technical rehearsals are held, testing each circuit and camera. At this stage some cabling often needs replacing – just one of the reasons it is not buried underground. The BBC takes its own power units with it – relying on the local electricity supply would be too difficult in terms of getting enough power in. An OB unit, on-air, consumes about 500 kilowatts of power.

Wednesday, normally pro-am day when the professionals are getting a practice round with assorted amateurs, is full rehearsal day, all cameras in operation for a dummy run of about an hour or so. This is when the action switches from the hustle and bustle on the course to the seemingly tranquil setting of the 'Starship Enterprise' – a 40ft-long trailer almost bursting at the seams with close to £3 million worth of electronic hardware.

This trailer, more correctly called the CMCCR (Central Mobile Colour Control Room), is a mini-studio all on its own, with banks of television monitors receiving pictures from every camera on the course together with graphics captions supplied by the Hewlett-Packard van parked right outside, plus a full sound studio and

Inside the 'Starship Enterprise' – a bank of TV monitors allows the producer to see almost every part of the course simultaneously.

Despite the impressive array of gadgetry, an efficient hum of activity is normally all you hear when the team is on the air.

Commentator Alex Hay describes the scene and the shot – even though he is actually far away from the action.

links to the commentators, sitting in their own mobile studio on the other side of the parking lot.

Contrary to popular belief, the commentators are nowhere near the golf course itself, watching the action on television monitors in front of them and linked to the director by radio.

BBC Television's Clive Clark out on the course.

Roving cameras bring a further dimension to golf coverage. BBC TV has now developed a remote camera which transmits directly rather than using leads like this one in the United States.

Their skill in assessing a good lie or a particular length of shot comes from years of experience in golf (both Peter Alliss and Alex Hay have played at the highest level) but they do have a handful of 'spotters' out on the course, feeding back information on such items as distance left, wind direction and the one everyone seems to want to know – what club did he use?

That information is passed by the player's caddy to the spotter, who whispers quietly into Peter Alliss's ear from afar via the director. The caddy has to make sure his player's opponent does not see or hear this information, of course, for that would incur a two-stroke penalty.

Thursday – if the event is being covered on all four days – is the big day, with live coverage beginning in mid-morning. Unlike some other sporting events such as motor racing, football and horse racing, precise timing of the first pictures is not critical. There is, after all, no kick-off time as such. So if a previous programme overruns a few minutes there is no sense of panic in the CMCCR.

The executive producer has overall control of the programme, deciding the format it should take and which golfers should be covered. Basically these are the leaders, any player with a high local interest (that was shown by the viewing figures of eight million when Faldo won the Open in 1990 compared to only five million when Ian Baker-Finch won in 1991) and, of course, the superstars such as Ballesteros, Stewart, Woosnam and Faldo.

John Shrewsbury explains his extra coverage of these by pointing out that the largest galleries always follow these players and television is just reflecting general public interest. On the early days of a tournament, before the halfway cut, the draw is made with television coverage in mind, ensuring that those golfers who attract public and media attention are on the course during prime coverage time, whilst trying to be fair to all the players. As most of the public galleries are on the course in mid-afternoon, too, this gives the spectators good games to follow.

Sitting next to the executive producer is Alastair Scott, an enthusiastic golfer like Shrewsbury – both insist they could not do their job as well if they did not play – who looks after the particular camera shots and mixes, talking constantly to all the cameraman out on the course

plus the mobile cameras, which are cable-free and able to roam at will, transmitting their images back to an electronically-equipped buggy, which in turn transmits them back to the control unit.

The commentators also take their cues from Scott, going back to a slow-motion repeat of a particular shot or looking at an overlay graphic of the leader board, the way a particular hole has been playing, or the scorecard of a player being featured.

Sitting next to Alex Hay in the commentary studio is Steve Rider who has next to him a fixed camera in a mini-studio, where prominent golfers are brought to be interviewed live after their round.

In another trailer a VT (video tape) unit team have access to 'stills' and playbacks, which are often inserted into the programme to provide the mix which British viewers have come to expect.

Variety is the key, with shots from all the leading players being the main ingredient of good golf coverage. The BBC golf unit can cover about six players pretty comprehensively, together with occasional shots from many more players. On short holes where a hole-in-one is possible, a camera is running throughout the tournament to capture that rare moment of triumph.

On an average tournament day, 4500 shots are played; television can capture about 10% of those. It becomes easier if there are only two or three golfers in contention for the lead. If someone makes a sudden break from a pack of followers, life becomes fraught in the 'Starship Enterprise', yet not so much as in the past. Nowadays, with excellent access to computerised scoreboards giving up-to-the-second information, any player making a break can be spotted immediately.

Audiences throughout the world vary in their tastes. In America commercial pressures compel the TV companies to show shot after shot after shot, with almost no break in between – apart from commercials. Britain shows the slower build-up: a player lining up a putt or clearly thinking about his shot. In America the theory is that in the few seconds that the player is lining up a putt, the viewer would have grown bored and switched channels – a highly contentious argument that has its supporters and detractors.

Up to eight million people in Great Britain alone watch the British Open. Pictures go to over 20 countries around the world.

Whatever the taste of a particular national audience, though, there are still the basics to contend with: showing the important golf shots. The crew who sit in front of two dozen monitors seeking out good pictures and exciting moments go about their jobs in a highly professional manner.

Yet in those last few countdown seconds before a linkman back at the Television Centre in London says, 'And now over to Steve Rider at the Open,' there is, in that quietly humming trailer, a sense of tingling expectancy. Another show is on the road.

RESULTS APPENDIX

British Open

Year	Winner	Venue	Score
			(over 36 holes)
1860	W Park	Prestwick	174
1861	T Morris Snr	Prestwick	163
1862	T Morris Snr	Prestwick	163
1863	W Park	Prestwick	168
1864	T Morris Snr	Prestwick	167
1865	A Strath	Prestwick	162
1866	W Park	Prestwick	169
1867	T Morris Snr	Prestwick	170
1868	T Morris Jnr	Prestwick	157
1869	T Morris Jnr	Prestwick	154
1870	T Morris Jnr	Prestwick	149
1871	No Championship		
1872	T Morris Jnr	Prestwick	166
1873	T Kidd	St Andrews	179
1874	M Park	Musselburgh	159
1875	W Park	Prestwick	166
1876	B Martin	St Andrews	176†
1877	J Anderson	Musselburgh	160
1878	J Anderson	Prestwick	157
1879	J Anderson	St Andrews	169
1880	B Ferguson	Musselburgh	162
1881	B Ferguson	Prestwick	170
1882	B Ferguson	St Andrews	171
1883	W Fernie	Musselburgh	159*
1884	J Simpson	Prestwick	160
1885	B Martin	St Andrews	171
1886	D Brown	Musselburgh	157
1887	W Park Jnr	Prestwick	161
1888	J Burns	St Andrews	171
1889	W Park Jnr	Musselburgh	155*
1890	J Ball (amateur)	Prestwick	164
1891	H Kirkaldy	St Andrews	166
			(over 72 holes)
1892	H Hilton (amateur)	Muirfield	305
1893	W Auchterlonie	Prestwick	322
1894	JH Taylor	Sandwich	326
1895	JH Taylor	St Andrews	322
1896	H Vardon	Muirfield	316*
1897	H Hilton (amateur)	Hoylake	314
1898	H Vardon	Prestwick	307
1899	H Vardon	Sandwich	310
1900	JH Taylor	St Andrews	309
1901	J Braid	Muirfield	309
1902	A Herd	Hoylake	307
1903	H Vardon	Prestwick	300
1904	J White	Sandwich	296
1905	J Braid	St Andrews	318
1906	J Braid	Muirfield	300
1907	A Massy	Hoylake	312
1908	J Braid	Prestwick	291
1909	JH Taylor	Deal	295
1910	J Braid	St Andrews	299
1911	H Vardon	Sandwich	303*
1912	E Ray	Muirfield	295
1913	JH Taylor	Hoylake	304
1914	H Vardon	Prestwick	306
1915–1919	No Championship		

Year	Winner	Venue	Score
1920	G Duncan	Deal	303
1921	J Hutchison	St Andrews	296*
1922	W Hagen	Sandwich	300
1923	AG Havers	Troon	295
1924	W Hagen	Hoylake	301
1925	J Barnes	Prestwick	300
1926	R Jones (amateur)	Lytham	291
1927	R Jones (amateur)	St Andrews	285
1928	W Hagen	Sandwich	292
1929	W Hagen	Muirfield	292
1930	R Jones (amateur)	Hoylake	291
1931	T Armour	Carnoustie	296
1932	G Sarazen	Sandwich	283
1933	D Shute	St Andrews	292*
1934	TH Cotton	Sandwich	283
1935	A Perry	Muirfield	283
1936	AH Padgham	Hoylake	287
1937	TH Cotton	Carnoustie	290
1938	R Whitcombe	Sandwich	295
1939	R Burton	St Andrews	290
1940–1945	No Championship		
1946	S Snead	St Andrews	290
1947	F Daly	Hoylake	293
1948	TH Cotton	Muirfield	284
1949	AD Locke	Sandwich	283*
1950	AD Locke	Troon	279
1951	M Faulkner	Portrush	285
1952	AD Locke	Lytham	287
1953	B Hogan	Carnoustie	282
1954	P Thomson	Birkdale	283
1955	P Thomson	St Andrews	281
1956	P Thomson	Hoylake	286
1957	AD Locke	St Andrews	279
1958	P Thomson	Lytham	278*
1959	G Player	Muirfield	284
1960	K Nagle	St Andrews	278
1961	A Palmer	Birkdale	284
1962	A Palmer	Troon	276
1963	RJ Charles	Lytham	277*
1964	A Lema	St Andrews	279
1965	P Thomson	Birkdale	285
1966	J Nicklaus	Muirfield	282
1967	R de Vincenzo	Hoylake	278
1968	G Player	Carnoustie	289
1969	A Jacklin	Lytham	280
1970	J Nicklaus	St Andrews	283*
1971	L Trevino	Birkdale	278
1972	L Trevino	Muirfield	278
1973	T Weiskopf	Troon	276
1974	G Player	Lytham	282
1975	T Watson	Carnoustie	279*
1976	J Miller	Birkdale	279
1977	T Watson	Turnberry	268
1978	J Nicklaus	St Andrews	281
1979	S Ballesteros	Lytham	283
1980	T Watson	Muirfield	271
1981	W Rogers	Sandwich	276
1982	T Watson	Troon	284

Year	Winner	Venue	Score
1983	T Watson	Birkdale	275
1984	S Ballesteros	St Andrews	276
1985	A Lyle	Sandwich	282
1986	G Norman	Turnberry	280
1987	N Faldo	Muirfield	279
1988	S Ballesteros	Lytham	273
1989	M Calcavecchia	Troon	275*
1990	N Faldo	St Andrews	270
1991	I Baker-Finch	Birkdale	272

* After a play-off

† In 1876 David Strath tied with Bob Martin but refused to take part in a play-off – Martin was declared the winner by default.

Most Wins: H Vardon (6), JH Taylor, J Braid, P Thomson, T Watson (5)

Most Second Placings: J Nicklaus (7)

Lowest Winning Score (over 72 holes): 268 (T Watson, Turnberry, 1977)

Highest Winnng Score (over 72 holes): 326 (JH Taylor, Sandwich, 1894)

Most Popular Winning Score: 283 (seven times)

US Open

Year	Winner	Venue	Score
			(over 36 holes)
1895	H Rawlins	Newport, RI	173
1896	J Foulis	Shinnecock Hills, NY	152
1897	J Lloyd	Chicago, Ill	162
			(over 72 holes)
1898	F Herd	Myopia, Mass.	328
1899	W Smith	Baltimore, Md.	315
1900	H Vardon	Chicago, Ill.	313
1901	W Anderson	Myopia, Mass.	331
1902	L Auchterlonie	Garden City, NY	307
1903	W Anderson	Baltusrol, NJ	307
1904	W Anderson	Glen View, Ill.	303
1905	W Anderson	Myopia, Mass.	314
1906	A Smith	Onwentsia, Ill.	295
1907	A Ross	Philadelphia, Pa.	302
1908	F McLeod	Myopia, Mass.	322
1909	G Sargent	Englewood, NY	290
1910	A Smith	Philadelphia, Pa.	298*
1911	J McDermott	Chicago, Ill.	307
1912	J McDermott	Buffalo, NY	294
1913	F Ouimet (am)	Brookline, Mass.	304*
1914	W Hagen	Midlothian, Ill.	290
1915	J Travers (am)	Baltusrol, NJ	297
1916	C Evans Jr (am)	Minikahda, Minn.	286
1917–1918 No Championship			
1919	W Hagen	Brae Burn, Mass.	301
1920	E Ray	Inverness, Ohio	295
1921	J Barnes	Columbia, Md.	289
1922	G Sarazen	Stokie, Ill.	288
1923	R Jones (am)	Inwood, NY	296*
1924	C Walker	Oakland Hills, Mich.	297
1925	W McFarlane	Worcester, Mass.	291
1926	R Jones (am)	Scioto, Ohio	293
1927	T Armour	Oakmont, Pa.	301*
1928	J Farrell	Olympia Fields, Ill.	294*
1929	R Jones (am)	Winged Foot, NY	294*

Year	Winner	Venue	Score
1930	R Jones (am)	Interlachen, Minn.	287
1931	B Burke	Inverness, Ohio	292*
1932	G Sarazen	Fresh Meadow, NY	286
1933	J Goodman (am)	North Shore, Ill.	287
1934	O Dutra	Merion, Pa.	293
1935	S Parks Jnr	Oakmont, Pa.	299
1936	T Manero	Baltusrol, NJ	282
1937	R Guldahl	Oakland Hills, Mich.	281
1938	R Guldahl	Cherry Hills, Colo.	284
1939	B Nelson	Philadelphia, Pa.	284*
1940	L Little	Canterbury, Ohio	287*
1941	C Wood	Colonial, Texas	284
1942–1945 No Championship			
1946	L Mangrum	Canterbury, Ohio	284*
1947	L Worsham	St Louis, Mo.	282*
1948	B Hogan	Riviera, Calif.	276
1949	C Middlecoff	Medinah, Ill.	286
1950	B Hogan	Merion, Pa.	287*
1951	B Hogan	Oakland Hills, Mich.	287
1952	J Boros	Northwood, Texas	281
1953	B Hogan	Oakmont, Pa.	283
1954	E Furgol	Baltusrol, NJ	284
1955	J Fleck	Olympic, Calif.	287*
1956	C Middlecoff	Oak Hill, NY	281
1957	D Mayer	Inverness, Ohio	282*
1958	T Bolt	Southern Hills, Okla	283
1959	W Casper	Winged Foot, NY	282
1960	A Palmer	Cherry Hills, Colo.	280
1961	G Littler	Oakland Hills, Mich.	281
1962	J Nicklaus	Oakmont, Pa..	283*
1963	J Boros	Brookline, Mass.	293*
1964	K Venturi	Congressional, Md.	278
1965	G Player	BelleRive, Mo.	282*
1966	W Casper	Olympic, Calif.	278*
1967	J Nicklaus	Baltusrol, NJ	275
1968	L Trevino	Oak Hill, NY	275
1969	O Moody	Champions, Texas	281
1970	A Jacklin	Hazeltine, Minn.	281
1971	L Trevino	Merion, Pa.	280*
1972	J Nicklaus	Pebble Beach, Calif.	290
1973	J Miller	Oakmont, Pa.	279
1974	H Irwin	Winged Foot, NY	287
1975	L Graham	Medinah, Ill.	287*
1976	J Pate	Atlanta Athletic, Ga.	277
1977	H Green	Southern Hills, Okla.	278
1978	A North	Cherry Hills, Colo.	285
1979	H Irwin	Inverness, Ohio	284
1980	J Nicklaus	Baltusrol, NJ	272
1981	D Graham	Merion, Pa.	273
1982	T Watson	Pebble Beach, Calif.	282
1983	L Nelson	Oakmont, Pa.	280
1984	F Zoeller	Winged Foot, NY	276*
1985	A North	Oakland Hills, Mich.	279
1986	R Floyd	Shinnecock Hills, NY	279
1987	S Simpson	San Francisco, Calif.	277
1988	C Strange	Brookline, Mass.	278*
1989	C Strange	Oak Hill, NY	278
1990	H Irwin	Medinah, Ill.	280*
1991	P Stewart	Hazeltine, Minn.	282*

* After a play-off.

Most Wins: 4 – W Anderson, R Jones, B Hogan, J Nicklaus.

Most Second Placings: 4 – R Jones, S Snead, A Palmer, J Nicklaus.

Lowest Winning Score: 272 (J Nicklaus, 1980)

Highest Winning Score: 328 (F Herd, 1898)

Most Popular Winning Score: 287 (eight times)

US Masters

Played at Augusta National

Year	Winner	Score
1934	H Smith	284
1935	G Sarazen	282
1936	H Smith	285
1937	B Nelson	283
1938	H Picard	285
1939	R Guldahl	279
1940	J Demaret	280
1941	C Wood	280
1942	B Nelson	280
1943–1945 No Tournament		
1946	H Keiser	282
1947	J Demaret	281
1948	C Harmon	279
1949	S Snead	282
1950	J Demaret	283
1951	B Hogan	280
1952	S Snead	286
1953	B Hogan	274
1954	S Snead	289
1955	C Middlecoff	279
1956	J Burke Jnr	289
1957	D Ford	282
1958	A Palmer	284
1959	A Wall Jnr	284
1960	A Palmer	282
1961	G Player	280
1962	A Palmer	280
1963	J Nicklaus	286
1964	A Palmer	276
1965	J Nicklaus	271
1966	J Nicklaus	288
1967	G Brewer	280
1968	R Goalby	277

Year	Winner	Score
1969	G Archer	281
1970	W Casper	279
1971	C Coody	279
1972	J Nicklaus	286
1973	T Aaron	283
1974	G Player	278
1975	J Nicklaus	276
1976	R Floyd	271
1977	T Watson	276
1978	G Player	277
1979	F Zoeller	280
1980	S Ballesteros	275
1981	T Watson	280
1982	C Stadler	284
1983	S Ballesteros	280
1984	B Crenshaw	277
1985	B Langer	282
1986	J Nicklaus	279
1987	L Mize	285*
1988	A Lyle	281
1989	N Faldo	283*
1990	N Faldo	278*
1991	I Woosnam	277

* After a play-off

Most Wins: J Nicklaus (6)
Most Second Places: 4 – B Hogan, T Weiskopf, J Nicklaus
Lowest Winning Score: 271 (J Nicklaus 1965 and R Floyd 1976)
Highest Winning Score: 289 (S Snead 1954 and J Burke Jnr 1956)
Most Popular Winning Score: 280 (ten times)

US PGA

Up to and including 1958 the US PGA was a matchplay tournament.

Year	Winner	Runner-up	Venue	By
1916	J Barnes	J Hutchison	Siwanoy, NY	1 hole
1917–1918 No Championship				
1919	J Barnes	F McLeod	Engineers, NY	6 and 5
1920	J Hutchison	D Edgar	Flossmoor, Ill.	1 hole
1921	W Hagen	J Barnes	Inwood, NY	3 and 2
1922	G Sarazen	E French	Oakmont, Pa.	4 and 3
1923	G Sarazen	W Hagen	Pelham, NY	38th hole
1924	W Hagen	J Barnes	French Lick, Ind.	2 holes
1925	W Hagen	WE Mehlhorn	Olympic Fields, Ill.	6 and 4
1926	W Hagen	L Diegel	Salisbury, NY	4 and 3
1927	W Hagen	J Turnesa	Dallas, Texas	1 hole
1928	L Diegel	A Espinosa	Five Farms, Md.	6 and 5
1929	L Diegel	J Farrell	Hill Crest, Calif.	6 and 4
1930	T Armour	G Sarazen	Fresh Meadow, NY	1 hole
1931	T Creavey	D Shute	Wannamoisett, RI	2 and 1
1932	O Dutra	F Walsh	Keller, Minn.	4 and 3
1933	G Sarazen	W Goggin	Blue Mound, Wis.	5 and 4
1934	P Runyan	C Wood	Park, NY	38th hole

Year	Winner	Runner-up	Venue	By
1935	J Revolta	T Armour	Twin Hills, Okla.	5 and 4
1936	D Shute	J Thomson	Pinehurst, NC	3 and 2
1937	D Shute	H McSpaden	Pittsburgh, Pa.	37th hole
1938	P Runyan	S Snead	Shawnee, Pa.	8 and 7
1939	H Picard	B Nelson	Pomonok, NY	37th hole
1940	B Nelson	S Snead	Hershey, Pa.	1 hole
1941	V Ghezzi	B Nelson	Cherry Hills, Col.	38th hole
1942	S Snead	J Turnesa	Seaview, NJ	2 and 1
1943	No Championship			
1944	B Hamilton	B Nelson	Manito, Wash.	1 hole
1945	B Nelson	S Byrd	Morraine, Ohio	4 and 3
1946	B Hogan	E Oliver	Portland, Ore.	6 and 4
1947	J Ferrier	C Harbert	Plum Hollow, Mich.	2 and 1
1948	B Hogan	M Turnesa	Norwood Hills, Mo.	7 and 6
1949	S Snead	J Palmer	Hermitage, Pa.	3 and 2
1950	C Harper	H Williams	Scioto, Ohio	4 and 3
1951	S Snead	W Burkemo	Oakmont, Pa.	7 and 6
1952	J Turnesa	C Harbert	Big Spring, Ky.	1 hole
1953	W Burkemo	F Torza	Birmingham, Mich.	2 and 1
1954	C Harbert	W Burkemo	Keller, Minn.	4 and 3
1955	D Ford	C Middlecoff	Meadowbrook, Mich.	4 and 3
1956	J Burke	T Kroll	Blue Hill, Mass.	3 and 2
1957	L Herbert	D Finterswald	Miami Valley, Ohio	2 and 1
				(strokeplay)
1958	D Finterswald		Llanerch, Pa.	276
1959	B Rosburg		Minneapolis, Minn.	277
1960	J Herbert		Firestone, Ohio	281
1961	J Barber		Olympia Fields, Ill.	277*
1962	G Player		Aronimink, Pa.	278
1963	J Nicklaus		Dallas, Texas	279
1964	B Nichols		Columbus, Ohio	271
1965	D Marr		Laurel Valley, Pa.	280
1966	A Geiberger		Firestone, Ohio	280
1967	D January		Columbine, Colo.	281*
1968	J Boros		Pecan Valley, Tex.	281
1969	R Floyd		Dayton, Ohio	276
1970	D Stockton		Southern Hills, Okla.	279
1971	J Nicklaus		PGA National, Fla.	281
1972	G Player		Oakland Hills, Mich.	281
1973	J Nicklaus		Canterbury, Ohio	277
1974	L Trevino		Tanglewood, NC	276
1975	J Nicklaus		Firestone, Ohio	276
1976	D Stockton		Congressional, Md.	281
1977	L Wadkins		Pebble Beach, Calif.	287*
1978	J Mahaffey		Oakmont, Pa.	276*
1979	D Graham		Oakland Hills, Mich.	272*
1980	J Nicklaus		Oak Hill, NY	274
1981	L Nelson		Atlanta, Ga.	273
1982	R Floyd		Southern Hills, Okla.	272
1983	H Sutton		Riviera, Calif.	274
1984	L Trevino		Shoal Creek, Ala.	273
1985	H Green		Cherry Hills, Colo.	278
1986	R Tway		Inverness, Ohio	276
1987	L Nelson		PGA National, Fla.	287*
1988	J Sluman		Oaktree, Okla.	272
1989	P Stewart		Kemper Lakes, Ill.	276
1990	W Grady		Shoal Creek, Ala.	282
1991	J Daly		Crooked Stick, Ind.	276

* After a play-off.

Most Wins: 5 – W Hagen (matchplay), J Nicklaus (strokeplay)
Most Second Places: 4 – J Nicklaus
Most Popular Winning Score: 276 (eight times)
All Time Majors Winners
Most Popular Winning Score (all four Majors): 280 (18 times)
Lowest Winning Score **(all four Majors):** 268 (British Open, 1977)
Highest Winning Score **(all four Majors):** 326 (British Open, 1894)

Leading Major Winners

Name	Open	US Open	Masters	USPGA	Total
Jack Nicklaus	3	4	6	5	18
Walter Hagen	4	2	–	5	11
Ben Hogan	1	4	2	2	9
Gary Player	3	1	3	2	9
Tom Watson	5	1	2	–	8
Arnold Palmer	2	1	4	–	7
Bobby Jones	3	4	–	–	7
Harry Vardon	6	1	–	–	7
Gene Sarazen	1	2	1	3	7
Sam Snead	1	–	3	3	7
Lee Trevino	2	2	–	2	6
Seve Ballesteros	3	–	2	–	5
James Braid	5	–	–	–	5
JH Taylor	5	–	–	–	5
Byron Nelson	–	1	2	2	5
Peter Thomson	5	–	–	-	5
Jim Barnes	1	1	–	2	4
Nick Faldo	2	–	2	–	4
Ray Floyd	1	–	1	2	4
Bobby Locke	4	–	–	–	4
Old Tom Morris	4	–	–	–	4
Young Tom Morris	4	–	–	–	4

Only four players, Nicklaus, Hogan, Sarazen and Player, have won all four of the Majors, though in fairness, the players who were at their peak prior to 1930 would not have had a chance to compete in the Masters. Jim Barnes and Harry Vardon won all the tournaments open to them, as did Bobby Jones.

Ryder Cup

Year	Venue	USA	Britain
1927	Worcester, Mass.	9½	2½
1929	Moortown, Leeds	5	7
1931	Scioto, Ohio	9	3
1933	Southport, Lancs.	5½	6½
1935	Ridgewood, NJ	9	3
1937	Southport, Lancs.	8	4
1947	Portland, Oregon	11	1
1949	Ganton, Lincs.	7	5
1951	Pinehurst, NC	9½	2½
1953	Wentworth, Surrey	6½	5½
1955	Thunderbird, Cal.	8	4
1957	Lindrick, Yorks	4½	7½
1959	ElDorado CC, Cal.	8½	3½
1961	Lytham, Lancs.	14½	9½
1963	Atlanta, Ga.	23	9
1965	Birkdale, Lancs.	19½	12½
1967	Houston, Texas	23½	8½
1969	Birkdale, Lancs.	16	16
1971	St Louis, Missouri	18½	13½
1973	Muirfield, Scotland	19	13
1975	Laurel Valley, Pa.	21	11
1977	Lytham, Lancs.	12½	7½

Year	Venue	USA	Europe
1979	Greenbrier, W. Virg.	17	11
1981	Walton Heath, Surrey	18½	9½
1983	PGA National, Fla.	14½	13½
1985	Belfry, West Midlands	11½	16½
1987	Muirfield Village, Ohio	13	15
1989	Belfry, West Midlands	14	14
1991	Kiawah Island, SC	14½	13½

Curtis Cup

		USA	GB
1932	Wentworth, Surrey	5½	3½
1934	Chevy Chase, Md.	6½	2½
1936	Gleneagles, Scotland	4½	4½
1938	Essex CC, Mass.	5½	3½
1948	Birkdale, Lancs.	6½	2½
1950	Buffalo, NY	7½	1½
1952	Muirfield, Scotland	4	5
1954	Merion, Pa.	6	3
1956	Sandwich, Kent	4	5
1958	Brae Burn, Mass.	4½	4½
1960	Lindrick, Yorks.	6½	2½
1962	Colorado Springs	8	1
1964	Porthcawl, Wales	10½	7½
1966	Hot Springs, Virginia	13	5
1968	Co. Down, Ireland	10½	7½
1970	Brae Burn, Mass.	11½	6½
1972	Western Gailes, Scotland	10	8
1974	San Francisco, Cal.	13	5
1976	Lytham, Lancs.	11½	6½
1978	Apawamis, NY	12	6
1980	St Pierre, Wales	13	5
1982	Denver, Colorado	14½	3½
1984	Muirfield, Scotland	9½	8½
1986	Prairie Dunes, Kansas	13	5
1988	St George's, Kent	7	11
1990	Somerset Hills, NJ	14	4

Walker Cup

		USA	GB+Ire
1922	Long Island, NY	8	4
1923	St Andrews, Scotland	6½	5½
1924	Garden City, NY	9	3
1926	St Andrews, Scotland	6½	5½
1928	Chicago, Ill.	11	1
1930	Sandwich, Kent	10	2
1932	Brookline, Mass.	9½	2½
1934	St Andrews, Scotland	9½	2½
1936	Pine Valley, NJ	10½	1½
1938	St Andrews, Scotland	4½	7½
1947	St Andrews, Scotland	8	4
1949	Winged Foot, NY	10	2
1951	Royal Birkdale, Lancs.	7½	4½
1953	Kittansett, Mass.	9	3
1955	St Andrews, Scotland	10	2
1957	Minikahda, Minn.	8½	3½
1959	Muirfield, Scotland	9	3
1961	Seattle, Wash.	11	1
		(format changed)	
1963	Turnberry, Scotland	12	8
1965	Baltimore, Md.	11	11
1967	Sandwich, Kent	13	7
1969	Milwaukee, Wis.	10	8
1971	St Andrews, Scotland	11	13
1973	Brookline, Mass.	14	10
1975	St Andrews, Scotland	15½	8½
1977	Shinnecock Hills, NY	16	8
1979	Muirfield, Scotland	15½	8½
1981	Cypress Point, Cal.	15	9
1983	Hoylake, Lancs.	13½	10½
1985	Pine Valley, NJ	13	11
1987	Sunningdale, Berks.	16½	7½
1989	Peachtree, Ga.	11½	12½
1991	Portmarnock, Ireland	14	10

Ryder Cup – Individual Records

EUROPE

Name	Years	P	W	L	H	Record
Peter Alliss	1953–57–59–61–63–65–67–69	30	10	15	5	41.66
Seve Ballesteros	1979–83–85–87–89–91	30	17	8	5	65.00
Brian Barnes	1969–71–73–75–77–79	26	11	14	1	44.23
Maurice Bembridge	1969–71–73–75	16	5	8	3	40.62
Ken Bousfield	1949–51–55–57–59–61	10	5	5	0	50.00
Ken Brown	1977–79–83–85–87	13	4	9	0	30.77
Peter Butler	1965–69–71–73	14	3	9	2	28.57
José-Maria Canizares	1981–83–85–89	11	5	4	2	54.55
Howard Clark	1977–81–85–87–89	13	6	6	1	50.00
Neil Coles	1961–63–65–67–69–71–73–77	40	12	21	7	38.75
Eamonn Darcy	1975–77–81–87	11	1	8	2	18.18
Nick Faldo	1977–79–81–83–85–87–89–91	31	17	12	2	58.06
Bernard Gallacher	1969–71–73–75–77–79–81–83	31	13	13	5	50.00
Brian Huggett	1963–67–69–71–73–75	24	8	10	6	45.83
Bernard Hunt	1953–57–59–61–63–65–67–69	28	6	16	6	32.14
Tony Jacklin	1967–69–71–73–75–77–79	35	13	14	8	48.57
Mark James	1977–79–81–89–91	19	7	11	1	39.47
Bernhard Langer	1981–83–85–87–89–91	25	11	9	5	54.00
Sandy Lyle	1979–81–83–85–87	18	7	9	2	44.44
Christy O'Connor Snr	1955–57–59–61–63–65–67–69–71–73	35	11	20	4	37.14
José-Maria Olazabal	1987–89–91	15	10	3	2	73.33
Peter Oosterhuis	1971–73–75–77–79–81	28	14	11	3	55.35
Dai Rees	1937–39–47–49–51–53–55–57–59–61	18	7	10	1	41.66
Dave Thomas	1959–63–65–67	18	3	10	5	30.55
Sam Torrance	1981–83–85–87–89–91	21	4	12	5	30.95
Peter Townsend	1969–71	11	3	8	0	27.27
Harry Weetman	1951–53–55–57–59–61–63	15	2	11	2	20.00
George Will	1963–65–67	15	2	11	2	20.00
Ian Woosnam	1983–85–87–89–91	21	8	10	3	45.24

USA

Name	Years	P	W	L	H	Record
Julius Boros	1959–63–65–67	16	9	3	4	68.75
Mark Calcavecchia	1987–89–91	11	5	5	1	50.00
Billy Casper	1961–63–65–67–69–71–73–75	37	20	10	7	63.51
Gardner Dickinson	1967–71	10	9	1	0	90.00
Dow Finsterwald	1957–59–61–63	13	9	3	1	73.08
Ray Floyd	1969–75–77–81–83–85–91	27	9	15	3	38.89
Hale Irwin	1975–77–79–81–91	20	13	5	2	70.00
Tom Kite	1979–81–83–85–87–89	24	13	7	4	62.50
Tony Lema	1963–65	11	8	1	2	81.81
Gene Littler	1961–63–65–67–69–71–75	27	14	5	8	66.66
Larry Nelson	1979–81–87	13	9	3	1	73.08
Jack Nicklaus	1969–71–73–75–77–81	28	17	8	3	66.07
Arnold Palmer	1961–63–65–67–71–73	32	22	8	2	71.87
Gene Sarazen	1927–29–31–33–35–37–41	12	7	2	3	70.83
Jesse Snead	1971–73–75	11	9	2	0	81.81
Sam Snead	1937–39–41–47–49–51–53–55–59	13	10	2	1	80.76
Payne Stewart	1987–89–91	12	5	6	1	45.83
Curtis Strange	1983–85–87–89	17	6	9	2	41.18
Lee Trevino	1969–71–73–75–79–81	30	17	7	6	66.66
Lanny Wadkins	1977–79–83–85–87–89–91	30	18	10	2	63.33
Tom Watson	1977–81–83–89	15	10	4	1	70.00
Tom Weiskopf	1973–75	10	7	2	1	75.00
Fuzzy Zoeller	1979–83–85	10	1	8	1	15.00

Table shows all golfers who have played 10 or more Ryder Cup matches. 'Record' column shows points gained as a percentage of points available.

INDEX

Page references in italics denote illustrations.